D1015801

LIFE IN THE AFTERLIFE

LIFE
IN THE
AFTERLIFE

Tim
LaHaye

 TYNDALE HOUSE
PUBLISHERS, INC.
WHEATON, ILLINOIS

*Old Testament Scripture
references are quoted from
the King James Version;
New Testament references are
from the New King James
Bible unless otherwise
indicated.*

*Library of Congress Catalog
Card Number 80-50667
ISBN 0-8423-2192-6, cloth
Copyright © 1980
by Tim LaHaye.
All rights reserved.
First printing, July 1980
Printed in the United States
of America.*

CONTENTS

THE OUT-OF-BODY PHENOMENON

A friend of mine once observed, "What this world needs is a man who has returned from the dead. Then we would know what life will be like in the next world."

This man is not alone. There are millions who think the same way. In the last few years we have seen an increasing fascination with this subject. It has been given impetus by the amazing stories of individuals who were considered clinically dead but suddenly, to the amazement of their doctors, nurses, or family, seemingly came back to life. Their reports of life "on the other side" contain more excitement than the best science fiction novels. Actually, such stories have always persisted, but never before have they been given the respectability of documentation by members of the medical profession or the academic community.

Dr. Elizabeth Kubler-Ross, researcher on death and dying, has written several books on the subject. In one of them she emphasizes the importance of her research by stating, "The unraveling of the mystery of death is truly the key to the door of life, for death is the final human destiny. Whatever happens beyond the grave, whether it be 'something' or 'nothing,' reflects ultimate reality and gives us the context of ultimate meaning or absurdity in which we must live our lives."[1]

"Ultimate reality"—everyone is vitally concerned about that.

In fact, everyone has a vested interest in real life beyond death. That is why you are reading this book and why over a million people have read *Life After Life* by Dr. Raymond A. Moody, Jr., and *Beyond Death's Door,* by medical doctor Maurice Rawlings. The implications of these incredible personal narratives have occasioned a myriad of speculations concerning existence beyond the grave.

We shall examine the teachings of these books, but first let's consider some of the eyewitness accounts of life beyond death. Dr. George Ritchie tells the amazing story of his own brush with death in 1943 when he "left his body." As an Air Force private trying to get into medical school, he was struck by an illness. This caused him to collapse in the X-ray room, where he was eventually pronounced dead. He described in detail the trip he took in a "non-solid form" to Richmond, Virginia. He could see and remember people, but they could not hear or see him. He then encountered "Jesus," who took him on a spiritual tour, first to heaven and then to hell, where people maintained the same passions they had possessed on earth with one notable exception—they could not fulfill them. The people who impressed him most were the suicides who were always repeating, "I'm sorry," "I'm sorry," "I'm sorry."

Dr. Ritchie's resuscitation was as amazing as his experiences during his twenty-minute "death." The orderly asked the duty officer to "give him [Ritchie] a shot of adrenalin directly into the heart muscle," even though he had been pronounced dead a second time. It may seem unreasonable for a medical officer to accept such an unlikely suggestion from a private, but he did so—and Pvt. Ritchie's heart resumed beating. A few years later, while attending medical school in Richmond, Virginia, he and some other pre-med students were traveling through the city when he recognized a street he had seen in his "out-of-the-body" trip. At his insistence, they turned the car at one particular corner and drove to a bar he had visited on the "trip." He recognized it clearly as the same one he had seen and entered previously—even though he had never been to Richmond before the night of his "death." As nearly as he could estimate, he had traveled 1400 miles from West Texas to Virginia and back in less than twenty minutes.[2]

While I am familiar with the fact that publishers can become overly enthusiastic in their attempt to transform ordinary books into best-sellers, I cannot dismiss the incredible stories and "evidence" that Moody presents. A student whose grandmother had recently "died" stopped by his office after a philosophy class which had been on Plato's theories on immortality. The student narrated the amazing out-of-the-body experience of his grandmother, who revived to tell about it. It wasn't the story that gripped Moody so much as its similarity to one related by a clinical professor of psychiatry at the University of Virginia some years earlier. It seems that his professor colleague had died two times, ten minutes apart, reviving each time. The details of what happened immediately after the "death" experiences so paralleled those of the grandmother's story that Dr. Moody embarked upon a research project that now includes over 150 documented accounts.[3] He has discovered such a similarity in the stories that he has developed this interesting composite description.

A man is dying and, as he reaches the point of greatest physical distress, he hears himself pronounced dead by his doctor. He begins to hear an uncomfortable noise, a loud ringing or buzzing, and at the same time feels himself moving very rapidly through a long dark tunnel. After this, he suddenly finds himself outside of his own physical body, but still in the immediate physical environment, and he sees his own body from a distance, as though he is a spectator. He watches the resuscitation attempt from this unusual vantage point and is in a state of emotional upheaval.

After a while, he collects himself and becomes more accustomed to his odd condition. He notices that he still has a "body," but one of a very different nature and with very different powers from the physical body he has left behind. Soon other things begin to happen. Others come to meet and to help him. He glimpses the spirits of relatives and friends who have already died, and a loving, warm spirit of a kind he has never encountered before—a being of light—appears before him. This being asks him a question, nonverbally, to make him evaluate his life and helps him along by showing him a panoramic, instantaneous playback of the major events of his life. At some point he finds himself approaching some sort of barrier or border, apparently representing the limit between earthly life and the next life. Yet, he finds that he must go back to the earth, that the time for his death has not yet come. At this point he resists, for by now he is taken up with his experiences in the afterlife and does not want to return. He is overwhelmed by intense feelings of joy, love, and peace. Despite his attitude, though, he somehow reunites with his physical body and lives.

Later he tries to tell others, but he has trouble doing so. In the first place, he can find no human words adequate to describe these unearthly episodes. He also finds that others scoff, so he stops telling other people. Still, the experience affects his life profoundly, especially his views about death and its relationship to life.[4]

Everyone does not undergo exactly the same experience. In fact, Dr. Moody indicates that most people report between eight variations, the order of events differ with the individual narrator. A typical Moody story is of a woman who related the following:

About a year ago, I was admitted to the hospital with heart trouble, and the next morning, lying in the hospital bed, I began to have a very severe pain in my chest. I pushed the button beside the bed to call for the nurses, and they came in and started working on me. I was quite uncomfortable lying on my back so I turned over, and as I did I quit breathing and my heart stopped beating. Just then, I heard the nurses shout, "Code pink! Code pink!" As they were saying this, I could feel myself moving out of my body and sliding down between the mattress and the rail on the side of the bed—actually it seemed as if I went through the rail—on down to the floor. Then, I started rising upward, slowly. On my way up, I saw more nurses come running into the room—there must have been a dozen of them. My doctor happened to be making his rounds in the hospital so they called him and I saw him come in, too. I thought, "I wonder what he's doing here." I drifted on up past the light fixture—I saw it from the side and very distinctly—and then I stopped, floating right below the ceiling, looking down. I felt almost as though I were a piece of paper that someone had blown up to the ceiling.

I watched them reviving me from up there! My body was lying down there stretched out on the bed, in plain view, and they were all standing around it. I heard one nurse say, "Oh, my God! She's gone!" while another one leaned down to give me mouth-to-mouth resuscitation. I was looking at the back of her head while she did this. I'll never forget the way her hair looked; it was cut kind of short. Just then, I saw them roll this machine in there, and they put the shocks on my chest. When they did,

I saw my whole body just jump right up off the bed, and I heard every bone in my body crack and pop. It was the most awful thing!

As I saw them below beating on my chest and rubbing my arms and legs, I thought, "Why are they going to so much trouble? I'm just fine now."[5]

After reading over 100 stories told to excite interest in life after death, I turned to an amazing account preserved and recorded by Archie Matson in his book *Afterlife,* published by Harper & Row (1975). With his permission, I use the following portion of it as told to him by Mrs. Louise Eggleston about her husband, Aubrey, a leading Norfolk, Virginia, banker.

One afternoon some twenty-five years ago my husband came home from the bank a little early and said he had a spell of indigestion, and would go out and play a round of golf to work it off. It was worse when he returned a couple of hours later, but he said he would try again by going bowling with our son Laddie. So off they went. About ten P.M. they came in, Aubrey obviously in great pain and looking ghastly. . . .He said he would have to give in and that I could call a doctor. Aubrey was the kind of man who was never sick and never went to a doctor so while he went to bed I called a personal friend on the Church Official Board who happened also to be a heart specialist.

By the time the doctor arrived Aubrey was practically unconscious. After listening carefully with his stethoscope the doctor turned to me and said, "I'm sorry, Mrs. Eggleston, but it is too late. There is nothing that can be done. Your husband will be gone within half an hour."

"You mean, Doctor," I said, "that there is nothing that can be done medically to save my husband's life?"

"Yes, absolutely nothing." (Remember that this was back in the early thirties and that there have been many advances in handling heart attacks since then.)

"Well," I said, "if you have done all that you can, I'll do what I can."

"But you don't understand, Mrs. Eggleston. It is too late. There is absolutely nothing that can save him now. The main artery supplying blood to one side of his heart has burst. His heart is already gone for all intents and purposes. But I will remain with you until it is over. It can't be more than half an hour, and you would have to call me to come right back."

I went into the next room and phoned my prayer partner, explaining the situation and asking her to pray in her home as I would in mine, knowing that Jesus healed every soul who came to him in any need, and giving thanks and visualizing my husband's perfect healing. We would continue thus to pray until we were given His peace.

One full hour passed before I felt that inner peace and knew that all was well. No sound had come from the next room and when I went in the doctor was sound asleep. I am confident that the Lord had to put him to sleep while He healed the patient. In order not to embarrass the doctor I called in and asked how my husband was coming along. You can imagine how chagrined the doctor was. He was even more surprised when he discovered Aubrey was not only alive, but his heartbeat was much stronger. He simply could not understand how this could be.

Well, to make a long story short, Aubrey was completely restored in a matter of two weeks or so, and lived for eighteen years more, the most active and useful of his entire life. He even took part in state golf tournaments, and worked long hours especially during the war when we were short of help, heading up the Norfolk area war loan drives, and carrying his full load in all church work.

But he was not the same man. He had died and gone into the next life where he was met by many of his loved ones who had passed over before him. He now knew from personal experience the wonder and glory of heaven. Always he had been a Christian and a loyal member of the church, active especially in its business affairs. However, he would never go to a funeral or take part in any discussion of death. These simply were not for him because of several tragic experiences with death in his boyhood. But now he knew the truth and had lost all fear. All during the war there was nobody in Norfolk in such demand to talk with parents who had lost their sons. He could bring real comfort because he knew what their boys were facing in the next life. He had been there.

So it was for eighteen years. Then he realized that it was his time to go. Laddie had been killed when a plane exploded in 1949, and Aubrey wanted to join his son in heaven. So he arranged his affairs and had his successor trained and appointed to take his place in the bank. Then he went with him to a meeting of the American Bankers Association in Detroit while I was leader in a healing camp in Pennsylvania. I came back just in time to drive out and pick them up at the airport, but instead, received an urgent message to come at once as Aubrey was in a Detroit hospital.

I got on a plane that night but it was five the next morning when I reached the hospital. As soon as my husband saw me he lay back in bed perfectly satisfied, and went into a light coma. The next hours were some of the strangest and most wonderful of my life. Aubrey was in two worlds at the same time. He was not only aware of me and talking to me, but he greeted by name some thirty or forty friends and relatives who were waiting for him. The last one was John Moreland, the poet, who had been best man at our wedding, and who had died unbeknown to him just two weeks before. It was a happy reunion![6]

Equally as startling is the same author's account of a woman named Natalie Kalmus, who reports about her sister.

Miss Kalmus had promised that no drugs would be administered to ease her sister's last hours because she was not at all afraid to die and was convinced that death would be a beautiful experience. Miss Kalmus describes the final scene:

I sat on her bed and took her hand. It was on fire. Then she seemed to rise up in bed almost to a sitting position.

"Natalie!" she said. "There are so many of them. There's Fred . . .and Ruth. . . .What's she doing here? Oh, I know!"

An electric shock went through me. She had said "Ruth." Ruth was her cousin who had died suddenly the week before. But she had not been told of Ruth's sudden death.[7]

Several years before Dr. Moody graduated from college, Dr. Karlis Osis, Research Director of the Parapsychology Foundation of New York, did extensive research into the area of unusual deathbed experiences. In a monograph published in 1961, entitled *Deathbed Observations by Physicians and Nurses,* he revealed some interesting details. He had sent a questionnaire to 10,000 doctors and nurses throughout the country, asking them about their patients' emotions, visions, or hallucinations at the time of death. Ordinarily such questionnaires are seldom returned by the busy members of the medical profession. But as an evidence of the interest in this field, 285 doctors and 355 nurses who estimated that they had attended 35,000 deaths returned theirs, indicating that 3,500 of their patients were conscious at death. (No doubt this number would have been greater before the many modern drugs that ease the dying process.)

Of the 3,500 conscious patients reported, 753 had pleasurable visions or experiences, and 1,370 claimed to have seen some kind of spirits. Thus over 40 percent of those who were conscious at death had some kind of premonition or vision, or a "body-leaving experience" at the time of death.[8] Most people tend to pass these events off as emotional or psychic phenomena induced by pain or the trauma of impending death. Others accept them as evidence of the existence of the soul/spirit of man that is the true seat of his identity.

Religion and Out-of-the-Body Experiences

It is interesting, though inconclusive, that of those reporting visions or out-of-body experiences in Dr. Osis's research, no one lacking religious faith or belief in immortality had visions of beauty or serenity. It is almost as if the unbelieving person is less apt to sustain a mind-relaxing experience at death than are believers.

Although Christians are usually quite reluctant to assign much importance to a death vision, or out-of-body experience, most of them know of some godly individual who was comforted at death by a vision of heaven. For instance, Dwight L. Moody (no relation to the *Life After Life* author), one of the greatest evangelists in Christian history, on a hot Sunday in New York in August, 1899, demonstrated his joyful anticipation of death.

Some day you will read in the papers that Moody is dead. Don't you believe a word of it. At that moment I shall be more alive than I am now. ...I was born of the flesh in 1837. I was born of the Spirit in 1855. That which is born of the flesh may die. That which is born of the Spirit shall live forever.[9]

Biblical Accounts of Death Experiences

No one who has read the text of Scripture can forget two outstanding out-of-the-body events. The New Testament tells the story of Stephen's matchless sermon, ending in his martyrdom. This sainted servant of God was not left to face death alone, however. "When they heard these things they were cut to the heart, and they gnashed at him with their teeth. But he, being full of the Holy Spirit, gazed into heaven and saw the glory of God, and Jesus standing at the right hand of God, and said, 'Look! I see the heavens opened and the Son of Man standing at the right hand of God!' Then they cried out with a loud voice, stopped their ears, and ran at him with one accord; and they cast him out of the city and stoned him. And the witnesses laid down their clothes at the feet of a young man whose name was Saul. And they stoned Stephen as he was calling on God and saying, 'Lord Jesus, receive my spirit.' And he knelt down and cried out with a loud voice, 'Lord, do not charge them with this sin.' And when he had said this, he fell asleep'' (Acts 7:54-60).

Since this is the record of the death of the first Christian martyr, Christians who believe in ''the law of the first mention''—that is, that when a teaching is communicated for the first time, it sets the pattern for its use throughout the Bible—have a right to expect similar experiences in death, particularly if they become martyrs. Very honestly, I have not been present at any martyr's death, but I have read many stories of such individuals being attended by angels or visions (see *Foxe's Book of Martyrs*). In addition, I have witnessed several Christians, facing death like D. L. Moody and my own grandmother, transported to the next world in peace.

Admittedly, such departures (including Stephen's) are hardly out-of-the-body experiences, but how else would you describe the apostle Paul's experience which most Bible scholars suggest occurred when he was stoned and left for dead in Lystra?

I know a man in Christ who fourteen years ago—whether in the body I do not know, or whether out of the body I do not know, God knows—such a one was caught up to the third heaven. And I know such a man—whether in the body or out of the body I do not know, God knows—how he was caught up into Paradise and heard inexpressible words, which it is not lawful for a man to utter. Of such a one I will boast; yet of myself I will not boast, except in my infirmities. For though I might desire to boast, I will not be a fool; for I will speak the truth. But now I forbear, lest anyone should think of me above what he sees me to be or what he hears from me. And lest I be exalted above measure by the abundance of the revelations, a thorn in the flesh was given to me, a messenger of Satan to buffet me, lest I be exalted above measure (2 Corinthians 12:2-7).

It is open to question whether or not this was Paul's personal out-of-the-body experience. He could be telling it about someone

else, but it is worded in such a way that most Bible scholars believe he was referring to himself. Whether it concerned Paul or
another, some suggest it is fascinatingly similar to modern out-of-
the-body experience stories.

All Out-of-the-Body Experience Stories Are Not Pleasant

While attending the Christian Bookseller's Convention last year,
I met Dr. Maurice Rawlings, a specialist in internal medicine and
cardiovascular diseases at the Diagnostic Hospital in Chattanooga,
Tennessee. He graciously gave me an autographed copy of his new
book (which has become a best-seller), *Beyond Death's Door.*
Dr. Rawlings became alarmed when he realized that Drs. Moody,
Kubler-Ross, Osis, Haroldson, and others leave the false impres-
sion that everyone who dies enters into pleasurable experience.

Since meeting him personally, I have seen Dr. Rawlings interviewed on national TV talk shows, sharing his personal testimony.
On one such show he brought the former patient who experienced
"going to hell."

This patient was a forty-eight-year-old white male who was a rural mail
carrier. He was of medium build, dark haired, and had a personality that
would please anyone. Unfortunately, he represented one of those rare
instances where the EKG not only went "haywire," but the heart stopped
altogether. He had a cardiac arrest and dropped dead right in my office.
Instead of fibrillating (twitching without a beat), the heart had just plain
stopped. He crumpled to the floor, lifeless.

With my ear to his chest, I could hear no heartbeat at all. With my hand
alongside his Adam's apple, I could feel no pulse. He gave one or two
sighing breaths before he quit breathing altogether. There were scattered
muscle twitchings and then convulsions. He was gradually turning blue.

Although six other doctors work as partners in the same clinic, it was
late afternoon and they had gone on to other hospitals to make evening
rounds. Only the nurses were left. But they knew what to do and their
performance was commendable.

While I started external heart massage by pushing in on his chest, one
nurse initiated mouth-to-mouth breathing. Another nurse found a

breathing mask, which made it easier to expand his lungs for him. Still another nurse brought the emergency cart containing pacemaker equipment. Unfortunately, the heart would not maintain its own beat. A complete heart block had occurred. The pacemaker was needed to overcome the block and increase the heart rate from thirty-five per minute to eighty or one hundred per minute.

I had to insert a pacemaker wire into the large vein beneath the collarbone which leads directly to the heart. One end of this electric wire was manipulated through the venous system and left dangling inside the heart. The other end was attached to a small battery-powered gadget that regulates the heartbeat and overcomes the heart block.

The patient began "coming to." But whenever I would reach for instruments or otherwise interrupt my compression of his chest, the patient would again lose consciousness, roll his eyes upward, arch his back in mild convulsion, stop breathing, and die once more.

Each time he regained heartbeat and respiration, the patient screamed, "I am in hell!" He was terrified and pleaded with me to help him. I was scared to death. In fact, this episode literally scared the hell out of me! It terrified me enough to write this book.

He then issued a very strange plea: "Don't stop!" You see, the first thing most patients I resuscitate tell me, as soon as they recover consciousness, is "Take your hands off my chest; you're hurting me!" I am big and my method of external heart massage sometimes fractures ribs. But this patient was telling me, "Don't stop!"

Then I noticed a genuinely alarmed look on his face. He had a terrified look worse than the expression seen in death! This patient had a grotesque grimace expressing sheer horror! His pupils were dilated, and he was perspiring and trembling—he looked as if his hair was "on end."

Then still another strange thing happened. He said, "Don't you understand? I am in hell. Each time you quit I go back to hell! Don't let me go back to hell!"

Being accustomed to patients under this kind of emotional stress, I dismissed his complaint and told him to keep his "hell" to himself. I remember telling him, "I'm busy. Don't bother me about your hell until I finish getting this pacemaker into place."

But the man was serious, and it finally occurred to me that he was indeed in trouble. He was in a panic, like I had never seen before. As a result, I started working feverishly and rapidly. By this time the patient had experienced three or four episodes of complete unconsciousness and clinical death from cessation of both heartbeat and breathing. After several death episodes he finally asked me, "How do I stay out of hell?"

I told him I guessed it was the same principle learned in Sunday school —that I guessed Jesus Christ would be the one whom you would ask to save you.

Then he said, "I don't know how. Pray for me."

Pray for him! What nerve! I told him I was a doctor, not a preacher.

"Pray for me!" he repeated.

I knew I had no choice. It was a dying man's request. So I had him repeat the words after me as we worked—right there on the floor. It was a very simple prayer because I did not know much about praying. It went something like this:

> Lord Jesus, I ask you to keep me out of hell.
> Forgive my sins.
> I turn my life over to you.
> If I die, I want to go to heaven.
> If I live, I'll be "on the hook" forever.

The patient's condition finally stabilized, and he was transported to a hospital. I went home, dusted off the Bible, and started reading it. I had to find out exactly what hell was supposed to be like. I had always dealt with death as a routine occurrence in my medical practice, regarding it as an extinction with no need for remorse or apprehension. Now I was convinced there was something about this life after death business after all. All of my concepts needed revision. I needed to find out more. It was like finding another piece in the puzzle that supports the truth of the Scriptures. I was discovering that the Bible was not merely a history book. Every word was turning out to be true. I decided I had better start reading it very closely.[10]

To his amazement, when he went to that patient two days later with pad and pencil to write down his recollections of being in hell, the man replied, "What hell? I don't recall any hell." Even under prompting, the man could not remember the entire horrifying experience. That is when Dr. Rawlings began to develop the theory, subsequently supported by many other case studies, that those who go to hell during out-of-the-body experiences or visions (or whatever these phenomena are) have such horrifying experiences that conscious minds blot them from remembrance. As you know, self-preservation is the first law of life. That is as true mentally as it is physically. The subconscious mind has a way of blocking out the unpleasant thoughts of life (unless the individual sadistically recites them on the conscious level). In the face of traumatic or terrifying experiences, this is often necessary to preserve mental health.

Dr. Rawlings points out that the thanatologist researchers (thanatology relates to death and dying) have rarely, if ever, interviewed patients at the time of their resuscitation, and most of the accounts studied are secondhand or years removed from the event. This is confirmed by Dr. Raymond Moody's admission that 100 of his 150 cases were interviews passed on by other doctors, and none of his own interviews closely approximated the experience.[11] Consequently, no valid conclusions can be drawn from his findings due to the memory rejection patterns of the subconscious.

Out-of-the-Body Experiences Are Not New

Most of us never heard of out-of-the-body experiences until these new thanatologists started giving them the respectability of scientific research and the media began to broadcast their findings. But really, such reports are not new. In fact, similar claims go back to the dawn of human history, some originating in the Orient and India.

The new breed of thanatologist is narrating events which are strangely similar to "astro-travel," "soul-projection," "astro-projection," or "Eckankar," the latter of which admits to being an occult experience. The major difference seems to be that the thanatologists' accounts are triggered by an accident or "sudden death" experience from which the patient recovered. Evidently, what astro-projectionists or "travelers" can do at will may also be triggered by the cessation of certain bodily functions, severe emotional trauma, or other mysterious forces within the mind.

Later in this book I will offer an explanation as to how this phenomenon occurs, but here I would like to acquaint you with some of the long-standing reports of out-of-the-body experiences that parallel those of Moody, Kubler-Ross and others.

Astro-Travel

One man, Ed Morell, was confined for four years within an Arizona penitentiary where he was subjected to torture resembling that of the Spanish Inquisition. He somehow learned to project his soul/spirit out of his body and was able to watch his tormentors. He also would travel throughout the state, which gave him access to information, reported upon his release, which could not have been known to him on any other basis. An interesting highlight of this story, written into a novel by Jack London, was that he could later only induce such out-of-the-body travel when under excruciating torture.

Space does not permit the inclusion of all the stories I have read concerning astro-travel that so resemble thanatology's out-of-the-body experiences. Besides, their authenticity is open to question. My only point is that when similar reports from totally unrelated areas of the world, covering almost four thousand years of human history, are put together, they not only resemble each other but bear a strange similarity to modern death and dying reports.

As could be expected, "astro-travel" can be traced back to the beginnings of Persia. Such Indian mystics as Shams-1 Tabrizor and Maulana Rumi, and Hindu mystics Tulsi Das, Guru Nanak, Sardar Singh, and many others were famous for it. They even had schools for teaching the practice. Alexander the Great, it is claimed by "soul travelers," performed his feats of conquering numerically superior armies by possessing the ability to leave his body at will and view the enemy force's encampments (an advanced form of aerial photography).

Such devotees are familiar with the names of Madame Blavatsky, one of the world's best known occultists; Zoroaster, who founded the Parsee faith; Mohammed, whose followers have massacred millions who stood in their way; Hafiz, a fourteenth-century poet of Persia; St. Anthony of Padua, a twelfth-century French monk; and before his martyrdom in 1170, Thomas à Becket. African tribes are still known to practice out-of-the-body transport, and it is presently the "ultimate" quality found in witch doctors. Afghanistan and the mountains of Tibet are replete with such stories. It is said that most of the Dalai Lamas have been adept at this "spiritual phenomenon." Most of the thanatologists' writings quote admiringly from the Tibetan religious writings.

One of the best known soul travelers was Emmanuel Swedenborg, labeled a "saint" or "guru" by many but an "apostate heretic" by Christians everywhere. Born in Stockholm in 1688, he has been called the "most remarkable projectionist in all religious history." He claimed to visit the dead, make trips to heaven and hell, and visit the stars in the universe. An avid writer, he left twenty-five lengthy volumes about his trips to other worlds, some of which contain vivid descriptions of how he saved people from hell or purgatory by taking them aboard a psychic elevator-lift type device that dropped them off in heaven. He felt that God had endowed him with the special ability of giving sinners a second chance after death. Anyone with even a little human kindness in his veins would cheer such a possibility—if it could be true. If it isn't, such a teaching could be deadly. You may be thinking, "Who would believe such a story?" Just millions of members of Swedenborgianism.

Satan Worshipers and Soul Travel

None of the modern thanatologists mentions that "soul travel," very similar in detail to some of their out-of-the-body experiences, is practiced by higher echelon Satan worshipers. Most thanatologist reports are of inexperienced soul travelers who were accidentally projected "out of their bodies," so they only cite one or two levels in the spirit world, though some have alluded to the various levels of life beyond death. This corresponds to the seven levels of Satanism, the seven levels of Mohammedanism (even the *illuminati* have seven levels for their initiates), and the various levels of Hinduism, reincarnation, and many others.

In his book, *The Satan Seller,* Mike Warnke relates a story much like the one he told my wife and me when we visited his home shortly after his conversion from Satanism. He had been a high priest. While awaiting orders from the "higher ups," he was alone in his room when a woman courier appeared from headquarters —hundreds of miles away. He talked with her, received his instructions, and watched her disappear—right through the locked door.[12] If that taxes your credibility, it is because you are (wisely) unfamiliar with such experiences, well known among Satanists, occultists, and mediums.

Several recent reports of out-of-the-body experiences have included individuals seeing their own "body" as an opaque or colorless gas-like substance which oozes out of their head (or feet), is transported away, and later returns when they are resuscitated. In the January 30, 1979, issue of *National Enquirer,* a college professor claims to have observed his wife's soul-spirit exit her body in a similar fashion. John Russell, of San Angelo, Texas, a former occultist and now a Christian, wrote to me recently:

Okay, to move on to "astral projection." The out-of-the-body experience is termed "astral projection" by the occult for the reason that a person is presumed to have projected his "soul" or "spirit" out of his physical body, and as a result is free to roam in whatever dimension of the spiritual world he desires, or, the "astral plane." In occult teaching, the "astral plane" is comprised of several different "planes" or "dimensions," which is how they give account for the many different experiences people have.

Let me substantiate that out-of-the-body experiences do indeed occur quite frequently in the occult, even without death. Some, rarely, are spontaneous. Most *are* premeditated. There are even schools that specialize in teaching many different techniques to attain astral projection. Experiments have been successfully done in which the projector would free himself of his body, go to a test site perhaps hundreds of miles away, identify previously unknown and random objects placed on a table, describe the people who were there and various other details of the test site, return to his body, call up the people by phone and name every item on the table accurately, name the people he saw there, etc.

Soul transport is not limited to official witchcraft or Satan worship. It is also practiced by mediums and other practitioners of the occult. A prominent garment manufacturer in Los Angeles told me that after taking Erhard's est training, he could project himself to other planets, where he had "seen the world as we look at the moon." (He did admit that he had to "quit that business after a year. I was flitting around the universe so fast that I was afraid of losing my mind.")

"Out-of-the-body universe travel" is not as obscure a claim as you might think. In fact, the great psychoanalyst, Carl Jung, even reported such an experience. In *Memories, Dreams, Reflections,* Susy Smith relates,

Jung had broken his foot and then had a heart attack. For some time he lingered between life and death, and it was then that he had a series of momentous nightly visions. "Once," he wrote, "it seemed to me that I was high up in space. Far below I saw the globe of earth, bathed in a glorious blue light. In many places the globe seemed colored, or spotted dark green like oxydized silver. Far away to the left lay a broad expanse —the reddish-yellow desert of Arabia. Then it was as though the silver of the earth had assumed a reddish-gold hue. Beyond was the Red Sea, and far, far back—as if in the upper left of a map—I could just make out a bit of the Mediterranean. . . ."

Jung estimated that in order to have had so broad a view of the world, he would have had to be a thousand miles up. "The sight of the earth from this height was the most glorious thing I have ever seen," he said.

Of the whole series of episodes Jung wrote: "It is impossible to convey the beauty and intensity of emotion during those visions. They were the most tremendous things I have ever experienced." Although he called them visions, he said of them, "I would never have imagined that any such experience was possible. It was not a product of imagination. The visions and experiences were utterly real; there was nothing subjective about them; they had a quality of absolute objectivity."[13]

You may be wondering about the connection between astral travel and out-of-the-body experiences as they relate to death. Well, consider the similarity of details. Some of those who have been catapulted "out of their bodies" have heard music, traveled down a long, dark tunnel, seen a bright light, met an all-loving personage, greeted friends and loved ones already dead, seen a playback of some of their life's experiences, flown out into space from which they saw worlds and stars and even "heaven," and reached a barrier from which they were forced to return. The conversations some report with "those gone before them" are similar to conversations with the dead claimed by modern mystics and mediums.

In his book already mentioned, Archie Matson shares an incredible experience with Los Angeles medium Arthur Ford (the same medium used by the late Bishop Pike, who carried on celebrated talks with his son after he committed suicide). Although out-of-the-body experiences (OBEs) were not involved, there were some uncanny similarities in communication with the soul-spirits of the dead. " . . .in the next life speech is not by sound, but by ideas, often in terms of symbols."[14]

All those quoted in Matson's book reported "good experiences" in the next life, the all-loving personage, etc. Similar to the OBEs, their spirit (who identified himself as "Fletcher") on the other side, the one who did the communicating, brought him a message from a minister friend whom he was surprised to find "up there" because he didn't realize he was dead—or even ill. When he checked his information, his colleague at that precise moment was in a coma. He concluded that the coma had enabled his minister friend to have an out-of-the-body experience so that when his medium called on soul-spirits, he could identify himself.[15]

Lest you think I am stretching Archie Matson's *Afterlife* with its joint-teachings of astro-travel, out-of-the-body experiences, medium communications, and automatic writing, listen to what Kubler-Ross says of his book on the front cover: "Will open new doors of thinking for the curious mind. Matson's findings coincide with our discoveries, and I am delighted that the clergy and scientists are beginning to help mankind overcome the still abnormal fear of death." Evidently she believes that Matson's brand of necromancy and mediumship "coincides" with their discoveries. I can't help wondering if that includes his doctrinal confusion such as advocating prayers for the dead, the idea of saints getting lonely in the next life, and the possibility that we may "sin and repent even after we have left our physical bodies."

Don't Be Confused

You are probably feeling a bit confused by the vague similarities between out-of-the-body experience research and the claims of the many ancient or modern groups cited here (which, by the way, are only the tip of the iceberg—many books recount such events). That shouldn't discourage you, for "life after death" is pretty heavy stuff. The variety of similar but often unrelated teachings on the subject not only emphasizes its complexity but signifies man's intense fascination with it.

In a future chapter, I will evaluate these modern out-of-the-body experiences for you and try to relate them to the real world. But first we should acquaint ourselves with the most complete and best teachings available today on life beyond death. Fortunately for us, God has not left us without adequate information on life in the next world. Admittedly, the Bible was not written primarily for that reason, but did you know that it mentions life after death in almost 1,000 verses? We won't study them all, but we will consider enough so that you will be equipped to make a proper evaluation of these popular teachings we have been considering and determine their true origin and meaning.

CHAPTER TWO

WHERE ARE THE DEAD NOW?

The most traumatic event in my life was my father's death three weeks before my tenth birthday. Until a person has gone through the tragedy of the loss of a close loved one, he rarely thinks about death. We tend to assume that life goes on forever, but real death destroys those illusions and creates questions that we have never before contemplated.

In my case, the first question I asked my mother was, "Where is Dad now?" That is probably the most commonly asked question under those circumstances, and not only by children. Everyone is curious about life in the afterlife. As far back as we can go in history, man has asked Job's classic question: "If a man die, shall he live again?" Life is so precious to human beings that the desire to live on in some future state is almost universal. Library shelves are filled with books on the subject, and practically every religion known to man offers some kind of teaching on the subject.

Looking back, I detect something interesting about my childhood reaction to my father's death that is common to many. At no time did I consider the possibility that he had ceased to exist, for my question indicated my assurance that "he" (the real person) was still alive somewhere. I just didn't know where. Fortunately for me (and certainly for my father), my parents had become Christians six years before he died. As I discovered later, that was the most important decision he ever made, for it determined where he spent his afterlife.

Due to that boyhood experience of death, I have studied the subject in great detail. My library is stocked with collections of books and articles on the subject from all over the world. It is my considered opinion that no one will be accurately informed on death until he studies the Bible's teaching and interprets all other writings (including the popular concepts mentioned in Chapter One) in light of it.

The next few chapters will define the basic scriptural teachings on life in the afterlife. Then we shall return to out-of-the-body phenomena to determine exactly what they really are and how they compare with the information given in the Bible.

The Bible is a book of life, not of death. Although it focuses extensively upon eternal and physical life, it also treats the subject of death many times. The sixty-six books of the Bible have much to say about death and the future life since God meant for man to know the truth. He knew that ignorance would arouse some of man's greatest fears. Yet when an individual knows God personally and is aware of what Scripture teaches about the afterlife, he is not afraid of death.

To get a comprehensive picture of God's presentation about death, we must turn to several books of the Bible and consider various references in the light of others, thus building a composite description. If you are fascinated by the subject of life in the afterlife, you will find our study most rewarding.

The World of the Dead

The thirty-nine books of the Old Testament refer to the world of the dead sixty-five times as "Sheol." The word may be translated as "the grave," "hell," or "death." Sheol must not be confused with "the pit" or "the lake of fire," for it is the place of all those who have departed this life, *both* believers and unbelievers. The New Testament word for this world of the dead is "Hades" (appearing forty-two times). It is important to note that "Sheol" and

"Hades" are not really "hell," as the King James version translates it. The Hebrew word "Sheol" and the Greek word "Hades" both refer to the same temporary place, whereas "hell" is a permanent place which lasts forever.

"Tartarus," a word that occurs only once in the entire Bible (2 Peter 2:4), is defined by Bible scholars as "the deepest abyss of Hades." Admittedly, we can't know much about that deep abyss, except that, as part of Hades, it too is probably temporary.

"Gehenna" is the New Testament word for the permanent Place of the Dead, used by Jesus Christ himself eleven times. James also used it (James 3:6). Of Hebrew origin from "valley" and "Hinnom," the word refers to the Valley of Hinnom, just outside Jerusalem, where the refuse of the city was dumped. It was characteristic of this valley that a fire was continually burning there. Many see this as a perfect characterization of hell—a place where "the eternal fire is not quenched" (Mark 9:48), or the "lake of fire" (Revelation 20:14), referring to the final place of dead souls that reject God.

The King James version of the Bible translates all of these words —Sheol, Hades, Gehenna, Tartarus—the same: hell. This leads to the confusing idea that they refer to the same place when actually they do not. Several modern versions have clearly distinguished among the words. The *New American Standard* version, for instance, calls the temporary places "Sheol" or "Hades," and the final place of the dead "hell."

A Description of Sheol-Hades

In order to gain a complete picture of the Old Testament teachings on the subject, we shall list some of the facts about Sheol—the temporary place of the dead.

Proverbs 9:18	A place where the dead exist.
Psalm 86:13	A place for the soul.
Psalm 9:17	A place for the wicked and those who "forgot God."
Genesis 44:29	Even a godly Jacob expected to go there.

Psalm 88:3	David expected to go there.
Psalm 89:48	All men will go to Sheol.

It seems quite apparent in the above verses that Sheol is a place where both the righteous and the wicked go immediately after death. It is a specific place and seems to be the dwelling place of the soul. Verse 15 of Psalm 49, "But God will redeem my soul from the power of Sheol" (NASB), indicates that the righteous expected one day to be released from Sheol.

Deuteronomy 32:22 and *Song of Solomon 8:6* mention a place where "worms cover" the wicked.

Ecclesiastes 9:10 describes a place where there is no "work," or "knowledge," or "wisdom."

Ezekiel 32:21 and *Isaiah 14:9, 10* speak of a place where conversation will take place.

Although there are many references to Sheol in the Old Testament, we need New Testament teaching to make the concept clear. As indicated in previous passages, it is evidently a place where both the wicked and the righteous go after death. However, the wicked suffer and are not promised eventual escape, while the righteous "rest from their labors" and are awaiting ultimate release.

The New Testament on Hades

The most complete description of Sheol-Hades in the Bible came from Jesus Christ himself (Luke 16:19-31):

"There was a certain rich man who was clothed in purple and fine linen and fared sumptuously every day. But there was a certain beggar named Lazarus, full of sores, who was laid at his gate, desiring to be fed with the crumbs which fell from the rich man's table. Moreover the dogs came and licked his sores. And it came to pass that the beggar died and was carried by the angels to Abraham's bosom. The rich man also died and was buried. And being in the torments in Hades, he lifted up his eyes and saw Abraham afar off, and Lazarus in his bosom. And he cried and said, 'Father Abraham, have mercy on me, and send Lazarus that he may dip the tip of his finger in water and cool my tongue; for I am tormented in this flame.' But Abraham said, 'Son, remember that in your lifetime you received your good things, and likewise Lazarus evil things; but now he is comforted and you are tormented. And besides all this, between us and you there is a great gulf fixed, so that those who want to pass from here to you cannot, nor can those who want to come from there pass to us.' Then he said, 'I beg you therefore, father, that you would send him to my father's house, for I have five brothers, that he may testify to them, lest they also come to this place of torment.' Abraham said to him, 'They have Moses and the prophets; let them hear them.' And he said, 'No, father Abraham; but if one goes to them from the dead, they will repent.' And he said to him, 'If they do not hear Moses and the prophets, neither will they be persuaded though one rise from the dead.' ''

It is important to note that this story is not a parable, but the record of a specific experience. Characters in parables are not given definite names but are identified as "a certain man," "a man," "a householder," etc. This story lists names—Abraham and Lazarus—as Jesus relates the factual record of two men who lived and died (possibly just prior to the narration of the story). They both went to Hades, but not to the same part. The chart on the next page will clarify our Lord's teaching on this subject and will serve as a basic guide to all the future events discussed in this book.

Three Compartments

It appears from this passage that Hades is composed of three compartments: Abraham's Bosom, the Great Gulf Fixed, and the Place of Torment.

The most desirable compartment in Hades, picturesquely called "Abraham's Bosom" or "Paradise," is a place of comfort. In verse 25, Abraham says of Lazarus, "now he is comforted." This would be the Paradise of the Old Testament to which the souls of the righteous dead went immediately after death. We can rightly assume that, like Lazarus, they were carried by the angels to this place of comfort. It is also a place of companionship for Lazarus, since he has the joy of fellowship with Abraham. No matter how he was treated on the earth, he now holds an enviable position by the side of Abraham. This, of course, introduces a wonderful

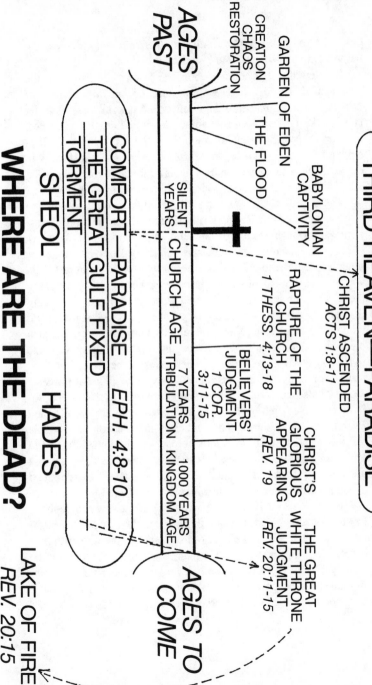

WHERE ARE THE DEAD?

THIRD HEAVEN—PARADISE

AGES PAST

CREATION
CHAOS
RESTORATION

GARDEN OF EDEN

THE FLOOD

BABYLONIAN CAPTIVITY

CHRIST ASCENDED
ACTS 1:8-11

SILENT YEARS

CHURCH AGE

RAPTURE OF THE CHURCH
1 THESS. 4:13-18

7 YEARS
TRIBULATION

BELIEVERS' JUDGMENT
1 COR. 3:11-15

CHRIST'S GLORIOUS APPEARING
REV. 19

1000 YEARS
KINGDOM AGE

THE GREAT WHITE THRONE JUDGMENT
REV. 20:11-15

AGES TO COME

SHEOL

HADES

COMFORT—PARADISE
THE GREAT GULF FIXED   EPH. 4:8-10
TORMENT

LAKE OF FIRE
REV. 20:15

possibility of fellowship with all the other saints of God gone on before: Elijah, Moses, David, and many others.

Very few details are given about the second compartment, the "Great Gulf Fixed," but we know that it is an impassable gulf over which men may look and converse but not cross. God designed it "so that those who want to pass from here to you cannot, nor can those who want to come from there pass to us." It is evidently a chasm that separates the believers and unbelievers in the next life. Once a person dies, he is confined to one side or the other—comfort or torment. (Some Bible teachers also believe that this Great Gulf has no bottom to it, and that it could well be the "bottomless pit" of Revelation 20:3 into which the devil is cast at the glorious appearing of the Lord Jesus Christ.)

More details are given about the "Place of Torment" than the other compartments. The Lord Jesus was clearly interested in warning men about this place in order to keep them from going there. The rich man called Hades a *place* of torments, indicating that it is a real place, not merely a state of existence, as some people would like to believe. Verse 22 tells us that "the rich man also died, and was buried"; verse 23 begins, "And being in torments in Hades, he lifted up his eyes." There seems to be no intermediary state, for the unbeliever goes immediately to the place of torment. Verse 23 also suggests that man is conscious of what he missed, for it states, "He lifted up his eyes and saw Abraham afar off, and Lazarus in his bosom." This indicates that one of the horrible tortures of Hades will be to look across the Great Gulf Fixed and view the comforts and blessings of those who are believers and are now comforted. The unbeliever will constantly be reminded of what he has missed due to his rejection of God.

It is impossible to be absolutely certain of the exact geographical location of Sheol-Hades. Some think it is in the heart of the earth, others that it lies in some undesignated spot in the universe. The Bible refers to it as "down" in Numbers 16:33, which might be responsible for the supposition that it is in the heart of the earth. Actually, the geographical location is not important. It is crucial, however, that this awful place of torment be avoided.

Escape from Sheol-Hades

One of the many outstanding changes wrought by the death, burial, and resurrection of Jesus Christ is that the believer has escaped from Sheol-Hades. Psalm 16:10, as quoted by Peter in Acts 2:25-31, establishes the fact that Jesus Christ is not in Sheol-Hades today. As the location of Hades is spoken of as "down," we find that in Acts 1:9 the Lord Jesus was "taken up, and a cloud received him out of their sight. And while they looked steadfastly toward heaven as He went up . . . ." 2 Corinthians 5:8 tells us, "We are confident, I say, and well-pleased rather to be absent from the body and to be present with the Lord." In other words, the believer at death does not go to Sheol-Hades, but is present with the Lord, who is not in Sheol-Hades because he dwells in heaven. In fact, the Scriptures teach that the Lord Jesus is presently "standing at the right hand of God" (Acts 7:55). Consequently, when a present day believer (or any Christian during the church age) dies, he no longer goes to Sheol-Hades, but his soul proceeds immediately to heaven to be with his Savior Jesus Christ.

One question naturally confronts us: "When did this change take place?" We know that the Lord Jesus went to Paradise, for in Luke 23:43 he told the thief on the cross who cried out for salvation, "today you will be with Me in Paradise." Therefore, we know that Jesus went directly from the cross into the Paradise section of Sheol-Hades. Now look at Ephesians 4:8-10. This passage reveals that Paradise is no longer located in Hades, but was taken by Christ up into heaven. This would indicate that the believer now goes to heaven, where he is joined with the Old and New Testament departed saints, leaving the former Paradise section of Hades an empty compartment. It is also very possible that at this time the Lord Jesus snatched the keys of Hades and death from the hand of Satan, for we see in Revelation 1:18 that he now holds them.

You are probably wondering why the Old Testament saints were directed to the Place of Comfort or Paradise in the first place. Why couldn't Daniel, David, Abraham, and all those great men and women of God go directly to heaven? After all, they believed in God while they lived. The answer is found in the inadequacy of the covering of their sins. In the Old Testament, sins were temporarily covered by the blood of a "lamb without blemish or without spot." But an animal's blood was not sufficient to permanently cleanse their sins (Hebrews 9:9, 10). Sacrifice was an exercise of obedience, showing their faith that God would someday provide permanent cleansing from sin through the sacrifice of his Son.

When our Lord cried from the cross, "It is finished," he meant that the final sacrifice for man's sin was paid. God in human flesh could accomplish what no animal sacrifice could ever do—atone for the sins of the whole world. After releasing his soul, Jesus descended into Hades and led all the Old Testament believers, held captive until sin was finally atoned for, up into heaven, where they are presently with him.

The Soulish State

We need to be careful not to confuse the present conscious state of the dead with the future resurrected state of the dead. The latter is described by Paul in 1 Corinthians 15, where he speaks of the rapture at which "we shall all be changed." Verses 52, 53 tell us that at the "last trumpet" the dead "will be raised incorruptible, and we shall be changed. For this corruptible must put on incorruption, and this mortal must put on immortality." Thus far the believer has not yet received his incorruptible resurrected body. That body will be described in detail in the next chapter, but for now, remember that it is distinctly different from the present *temporary* state of the dead.

The best term I know to describe this state is "soulish." Some call it a "soul-spirit" state, but I hesitate to use "spirit" because it is often confused with apparitions or spiritism. The "soulish state" then, describes the present condition of the dead. We have already noted that it was described by our Lord in Luke 16:19-33 as a condition of life that is quite different from that of our physical life. It is conscious and recognizable; it can converse and be comforted or tormented. Earthly events are remembered, and those who go to torment may not pass over into comfort. The Old Testament believers, as we have seen, have been taken by Christ up into Paradise, where they have been joined by the souls of Christians at death ever since the first century. The soulish state is both conscious and immediate upon death.

No Limbo or Purgatory

The soulish state should not be confused with the much-popularized "Purgatory" or "Limbo," which are not a product of the Word of God but a concept of the imagination of man. Purgatory is said to be a place where men go to do penance or suffer for the sins they have committed in this world in order to purify them for a better afterlife. The startling difference between the biblical presentation of the present state of the dead and this false teaching is that there is no indication whatever in the Bible that those in the torment section of Sheol-Hades or those in heaven will ever be anywhere but where they are for all eternity. We have already learned that anyone in the Place of Torment will never bridge the Great Gulf Fixed and gain Paradise. On the contrary, all those who are presently in torment will eventually be cast into the Lake of Fire. People are sent from this life into the Place of Torment because they have not accepted Jesus Christ and because their names are not written in the Book of Life (Revelation 20:12-15). The suggestion that those in torment today will be granted a later opportunity to be saved contradicts Isaiah 38:18, which says, "For the grave [Sheol] cannot praise thee, death can not celebrate thee: they that go down into the pit cannot hope for thy truth." The Place of Torment is strictly a place of suffering and is void of the teaching of truth. Therefore, those who enter that place cannot hope for escape. This is tragically true, but the tragedy does not lessen the truth.

The Way to Hades

The way to Hades is the way of neglect. The Bible tells us, "How shall we escape, if we neglect so great salvation?" A man winds up in Hades not because he is rich or poor, or because he is a murderer, a whoremonger, or a thief. A man is sent to Hades because he is an "unbeliever," because he has never accepted Jesus Christ as his own Savior. According to John 3:18, "He who believes in Him is not condemned; but he who does not believe is condemned already, because he has not believed in the name of the only begotten Son of God."

Note that both those who go to Paradise and those who end up in Hades are sinners. The latter die in their sins, while those who reside in Paradise were forgiven of their sins sometime during life. Jesus himself gave us clear directions on how to obtain admittance to this glorious place when he said, "I am the way, the truth, and the life. No one comes to the Father except through Me" (John 14:6). Only by Jesus Christ, then, can we gain access to the Father. Inasmuch as the Father is in heaven (where Paradise is located), it follows that only by Jesus Christ do we have access to heaven. On the contrary, all men deserve to go to hell (Romans 3:23, 6:23). Only through faith in the Lord Jesus Christ and his finished work on Calvary's cross can we escape Hades and hell. John 1:12 says, "But as many as received Him, to them He gave the right to become children of God, even to those that believe in His name."

The Message of Sheol

The message of Sheol-Hades can be put into one word, found in Luke 16:30. The rich man in Hades pleaded with Abraham that he would send Lazarus back to life to warn his five brethren. What was it that the rich man anxiously wished Lazarus to tell his brothers to do? The answer appears in verse 30—REPENT. For he said, "If one went unto them from the dead, they will repent."

If it were possible for a departed soul to return from Hades to give one last message to his living loved ones, it would be the same one which the rich man wanted for his brothers—REPENT. "Repent" that you might avoid this awful place. The greatest tragedy in the world is not that Jesus Christ was crucified on the cross, but that men and women have heard the message of his death to save them from Hades and hell, and have rejected it, refusing to repent and believe on him. In spite of the fact that he has died for them, they will spend eternity in torment. To activate the eternal effects of God's forgiveness of sins through the death of his son, everyone must call on the name of the Lord and be saved (Romans 10:13). There is no other way—and no second chance.

CHAPTER THREE

THE RESURRECTION OF THE BODY

Life after death is the universal thought, dream, or teaching of all mankind. Philosophies may be vastly different, but almost no one considers death the end of life. In Bombay, India, I saw hundreds of people wearing white masks over their mouths. These people, who called themselves Parsees, prayed for the dead, believing they would come back to life in other forms (depending on how they had lived: if a good life, in a higher caste of human; if a bad life, in the lower form of an animal or bug). The masks were worn to keep them from inadvertently swallowing their grandfather or other distant relatives.

Even attempted suicides have confided to me that their ultimate rationale was to find things better in the next life. Have you ever wondered why people universally hold onto this belief in resurrection or life after death? Could it not be intuitive with human beings? If so, God put it there; and if he did, we can expect the Bible to reveal unique insights about it. The careful student of the Scriptures knows that the Bible is not silent on this subject. In fact, it could well be called a book of resurrection. Christianity is built on the foundation of the resurrection of the body of Jesus Christ, and he promised his followers, "Because I live, you shall live also."

Space will not permit us to give all the biblical teaching on resurrection, but we shall provide ample references from both the Old and New Testaments to establish the subject as a fact.

The Old Testament

Job: The oldest recorded statement on resurrection came from the man who reflected the greatest understanding of God and his ways in the first two thousand years of human history. "For I know that my redeemer liveth, and that he shall stand at the latter day upon the earth: And though after my skin worms destroy this body, yet in my flesh shall I see God: Whom I shall see for myself, and mine eyes shall behold, and not another; though my reins be consumed within me" (Job 19:25-27).

David: The greatest king of Israel, known as "the man after God's own heart," said: "I will bless the Lord, who hath given me counsel: my reins also instruct me in the night seasons. I have set the Lord always before me: because he is at my right hand, I shall not be moved. Therefore my heart is glad, and my glory rejoiceth: my flesh also shall rest in hope. For thou wilt not leave my soul in hell; neither wilt thou suffer thine Holy One to see corruption. Thou wilt shew me the path of life: in thy presence is fulness of joy; at thy right hand there are pleasures for evermore" (Psalm 16:7-11).

Daniel: One of the three men called "righteous" in the Scriptures said, "And many of them that sleep in the dust of the earth shall awake, some to everlasting life, and some to shame and everlasting contempt" (Daniel 12:2).

Abraham: The venerated patriarch, referred to more in the New Testament than any other Old Testament saint, was said to have looked forward to living in "a city which hath foundations, whose builder and maker is God" (Hebrews 11:10). Obviously, he anticipated living after death in that city. Verse 19 makes it clear that he believed in the resurrection of the body.

Jewish Thought at the Time of Christ

Mary and Martha were products of Old Testament teaching at the time of Christ. When their brother Lazarus died, Martha's statement to Jesus shows how well entrenched in the Jewish thought of her day was belief in the resurrection. She said, "I know that he will rise again in the resurrection at the last day" (John 11:24).

Further evidence of Jewish belief in the resurrection appears in the conflict that existed between the Pharisees, who held to the resurrection, and the Sadducees, who did not.

Jesus on Resurrection

No one in the Bible spoke more about resurrection than Jesus Christ. That is not surprising, for he knew more about life beyond death than anyone else. After all, he created everything. Here is an incredible statement he made on this subject:

"Most assuredly, I say to you, the hour is coming, and now is, when the dead will hear the voice of the Son of God; and those who hear will live. For as the Father has life in Himself, so He has given to the Son to have life in Himself, and has given Him authority to execute judgment also, because He is the Son of Man. Do not marvel at this; for the hour is coming in which all who are in the graves will hear His voice and come forth—those who have done good, to the resurrection of life, and those who have done evil, to the resurrection of condemnation" (John 5:25-29).

Another was his comment to Martha about the death of Lazarus, "Your brother will rise again . . .I am the resurrection and the life. He who believes in Me, though he may die, he shall live" (John 11:23-25). He further elaborates on the subject by saying, "And whoever lives and believes in Me shall never die" (John 11:26).

Jesus obviously was not denying physical death here, for they stood at the tomb of his physically dead friend, Lazarus. Our Lord clearly meant that those who "believe" or have committed themselves to him may die physically, but the *real* person, the soul and spirit, would not die! As we have seen, it (the soul and spirit) goes to be with him in Paradise at death, until the resurrection of the physical body.

Christ spoke about the resurrection so many times that he could not be God in human flesh, as the Bible teaches, *if there is no resurrection;* for one characteristic of deity is accuracy. The resurrection of the human body and the deity of Jesus Christ are insepa- rable truths. In short, the resurrection of the human body is as certain as the deity of Jesus Christ, and that is as certain as his own bodily resurrection two thousand years ago, which is the most authentic fact of history.

The Universality of Belief in Immortality

Scoffers have suggested that a belief in life after death comes only from the Bible: if it weren't so widely taught, people would scarcely give it a thought. They are correct in saying that it is central to biblical teaching, but all the facts of history (particularly as seen in the testimony of archaeology) indicate that belief in life beyond the grave is universal. Ethnologists have yet to find a race without this hope.

In an attempt to prepare for the next life, the ancient Egyptians encased their kings' bodies in elaborate monuments called pyramids. The teachings of Plato, Socrates, and Aristotle demonstrate that Greek philosophers shared Job's concern over the question of future existence. The poetry of Virgil, Ovid, and Homer conveys the Roman belief in man's immortality. The American Indians' practice of burying their braves alongside their favorite bow and arrow testifies to their belief in life after death.

Every religion known to man establishes a place for the self after death. For the Hindus, it is called "Nirvana," entered by a series of reincarnations. Muslims get there by giving alms to "Allah," to whom they pray five times daily. Although this is a distorted view of the Bible's "heaven," it represents just one of the many expectations of people who are concerned about life after death.

How do we explain this universal belief in the future life? The only satisfactory answer suggests intuitive knowledge. Some things are known instinctively, and life after death is one. It seems that God designed into man's mental and psychic nature the realization of right and wrong (called conscience) and the intuitive knowledge that he will live somewhere forever. Temple ruins around the world present mute evidence that man is innately religious. This religious urge is definitely linked to his desire for life after death.

It has been suggested that this intuitive knowledge is God's appointed witness that we shall truly live again. In other words, since man possesses an "eternity instinct," that in itself indicates that there must be an eternity in which he can satisfy his longing. The Bible provides many fascinating details about the next life which man's intuition cries out for him to believe. Just as God satisfies all of man's other legitimate desires, he has given sufficient information in his Word to adequately fulfill that inner yearning for the truth about eternity.

Bible Teaching on the Future Life

The Bible is not the only book that teaches about the next life, but it *is* the only one that contains the standards of credibility. The mythological inconsistency of the others loudly decries their human origin. The Bible is quite different. It contains a dignity, consistency, and believability that would be impossible to achieve under human authorship. Compiled by forty-six different people writing during a period of 1,600 years, it confronts us with the miracle of its consistency and contemporary application. If such a book had been conceived by men, it would have become obsolete soon after it was compiled. Yet studying the Bible is still a stimulating challenge to the modern man. Why? Because of its divine authorship. Any question, any doubt, any thirst for knowledge can be satisfied by absorbing its contents with an open heart and mind.

Andrew Carnegie once offered a million dollars to anyone who could prove to his satisfaction that there is life after death. Like many others who claim to want that proof, he excluded the only real source of evidence, the Bible. Trying to learn about everlasting life without consulting the everlasting God is like trying to light the world without the sun. No wonder he died without the assurance of where he would spend eternity.

We could present many logical arguments and philosophical reasons to support the reality of life after death, but this, at best, is secondary evidence. Human reasoning and speculation are insignificant compared to the absolute truth revealed by the almighty

God. He has given us his Word to reveal the future. And that is enough.

The Fact of the Resurrection

There are numerous other references to life after death in the Old Testament. It was accepted as an undeniable fact in the minds of all the godly saints before Christ: Moses, Enoch, Jacob, Isaiah, Hosea, and many others. As we have noted, at the time of Christ widespread acceptance of a bodily resurrection is vividly revealed in a conversation between the Lord Jesus and Martha of Bethany. Her brother, Lazarus, had died four days before Jesus arrived at their home. He said to the sorrowing sister, "Your brother will arise again." When she replied, "I know that he will rise again in the resurrection at the last day," Martha reflected the faithful Israelite's attitude toward death and resurrection. It was common knowledge that godly people would be resurrected at the last day. This Old Testament teaching had a strong effect on people who for five centuries had lacked a prophet or message from God.

Some skeptics in that day did not believe in anything supernatural, including the resurrection. These people were called "Sadducees," a very small sect in Israel. I remember a Bible college professor who made an interesting play on their name: "Those skeptics did not believe in the resurrection. No wonder they were called Sad-You-See." His questionable humor notwithstanding, the point is well taken. Any man without hope beyond the grave is sad indeed, particularly when he is faced with the death of a loved one. Only a Christian can come out of that experience with a song in his heart. His joy in the face of sorrow can only be explained on the basis of his confidence in the resurrection.

New Testament Resurrection

As we have noted in the case of Martha, the Jews of Jesus' day had a deep confidence in the validity of the resurrection. This is evidenced in several other New Testament passages.

After King Herod had John the Baptist killed, the people showed their fear of God's judgment, for when they heard about the ministry of Jesus, their first reaction was to say, " . . .John had risen from the dead, and by some that Elijah had appeared, and by others that one of the old prophets had risen again" (Luke 9:7, 8).

Resurrection from the dead was well-accepted in our Lord's day, not only because it was a basic teaching in the Old Testament; but because they knew of several actual incidents of resurrection at the hands of the prophets. Elijah raised the son of the widow at Zarephath (1 Kings 17:21), and two were raised during the ministry of Elisha. The son of the Shunammite woman was returned to life (2 Kings 4:34) as well as the dead man whose body accidentally touched the bones of Elisha's body (2 Kings 13:21).

The New Testament documents many of its own case histories of resurrection. The Lord Jesus raised three: the widow of Nain's son (Luke 7:11-16), Jairus' daughter (Luke 8:41-56), and Lazarus, cited in John's Gospel, who had been dead four days. In addition, many saints were raised at the time of Christ's death (Matthew 27:52, 53). Then there is the case of Dorcas at Joppa, the benevolent disciple whom Peter raised (Acts 9:40-42). Paul preached Eutychus to sleep, but after the somnolent man fell to his death from his upper story window seat, the apostle prayed for him and he came back to life (Acts 20:9, 10).

All of these resurrections shared one common trait: the individuals did not remain physically alive forever. Although each one had his life span elongated, he ultimately died a natural death a second time. Thus, the resurrected ones await the final resurrection day for an eternal existence; extended physical life does not become eternal life.

Doctrinally and philosophically, Christianity rests uniquely on the resurrection of Jesus' body from the tomb. "What happened to the body of Jesus Christ?" is indeed *the* question of the ages. No one has ever claimed to have found it. Either it was stolen or he did in fact rise from the dead. Although there are many reasons for rejecting the first possibility, one stands majestically above the others: the people who were changed because of their contact with him. It was not the empty tomb that transformed the disciples from cowardly men into courageous heroes. That was the dynamic result of their individual confrontations with the risen Christ as he walked this earth, "appearing to many" during the forty days between his resurrection and visible ascension into heaven. Having seen and handled him during those days, they were never the same. That experience, together with the indwelling of the Holy Spirit, motivated them to turn the world upside down (Acts 17:6).

The guarantee of the Christian's eventual resurrection resides in the resurrection of Christ himself. He said, "Because I live, you will live also" (John 14:19). Therefore, the primary cornerstone in the foundation of Christianity, Christ's resurrection, is the guarantee of man's eventual resurrection.

It is impossible to separate a true preacher of the gospel and a preacher of the resurrection. In the first century, the two concepts were inseparably entwined. The fact of the resurrection appears in Peter's first two sermons, found in Acts 2, 3. This subject caused Paul's rejection by the Athenians when he preached on Mars Hill, for we read, "And when they heard of the resurrection of the dead, some mocked . . ." (Acts 17:32).

Not only in the sermons in Acts, but also in the thirteen epistles of Paul, we find frequent reference to the resurrection. To the Corinthian church, a people living in the heart of Greek mythology and religious confusion, he dedicated an entire chapter to the resurrection (1 Corinthians 15). To the Philippians, Paul said he was willing to experience the sufferings of Christ because he anticipated " . . .the resurrection from the dead" (Philippians 3:11). To Timothy he indicated that he expected a crown from Christ in the life to come—after the resurrection (2 Timothy 4:8).

The apostle Peter used the promise of the resurrection as a means of comfort in extending hope to the believers who were being persecuted for their faith in Christ. In 1 Peter 4:2-13, he encouraged the believers to rejoice in their present sufferings, "That, when His glory is revealed, you may also be glad with exceeding joy." In other words, to him present sufferings are insignificant when compared to the blessing which the believer will receive when Christ comes in his glory. This hope could only be realized by the resurrection of the body.

The book of Revelation reveals the culmination of all things. The beautiful description of the millennial kingdom, the new heaven, the new earth, and the eternal ages to come are all dependent on the resurrection of the body. If the fact of this resurrection were absent from the events prophesied in Revelation, the book would be reduced to a shallow remnant, robbed of some of the most vital truths of God.

Teachings of Jesus

We might ask the apostles, "Where did all this consciousness regarding the resurrection come from?" Even their traditional Jewish training could not account for it, because their knowledge far exceeded that of the typical Jew of their day. Once again, it was the influence of Jesus that separated these men from their contemporaries. Three years spent studying at the feet of the Master provided unlimited exposure to God's truths. Then, as now, one can only learn of God through his Son, who reveals him to us.

In Matthew 22:31, 32, Jesus presents a very startling teaching. "But concerning the resurrection of the dead . . .God, saying, 'I am the God of Abraham, the God of Isaac, and the God of Jacob.' God is not the God of the dead, but of the living." The Lord Jesus Christ, being God, knew his grammatical tenses. He did not say that God *was* the God of Abraham, Isaac, and Jacob. No, God *is*. At the time the Lord Jesus made this statement, these men were long since dead. Only resurrection could fulfill this statement.

His belief in the conscious existence of the soul after death and the ultimate bodily resurrection can be the only explanation for his astounding statement to Martha in John 11:25, 26. He not only claimed resurrection power for himself, but ultimately for all men when he said, "I am the resurrection and the life. He who believes in Me, though he may die, he shall live. And whoever lives and believes in Me shall never die. Do you believe this?"

The most absolute and dogmatic statement in the Bible regarding the resurrection came from the lips of the Lord Jesus Christ. It is found in John 5:25-29.

Most assuredly, I say to you, the hour is coming, and now is, when the dead will hear the voice of the Son of God; and those who hear will live. For as the Father has life in Himself, so He has given to the Son to have life in Himself, and has given Him authority to execute judgment also, because He is the Son of Man. Do not marvel at this; for the hour is coming in which all who are in the graves will hear His voice and come forth—those who have done good, to the resurrection of life, and those who have done evil, to the resurrection of condemnation.

This statement of assurance reveals many details about the resurrection not found in the Old Testament. For one thing, it becomes clear that Jesus Christ is the one who raises the dead with his voice. If his voice could call the worlds into being, and his word could raise Lazarus and others from the dead, we can be confident in his ability to raise us up.

The passage likewise explains that both kinds of people will be resurrected: "Those who have done good" (which is synonymous with receiving him by faith—the only thing man can do to please God); and "Those who have done evil" (those who reject him). There can be no question that Jesus Christ believes in and is responsible for the ultimate resurrection of the body and the eternal life it affords.

Resurrection and the Second Coming

The Second Coming of Jesus Christ is mentioned 318 times in the New Testament. Next to salvation, it is the most frequently mentioned teaching in the Bible. We are told that when Christ comes again, he is going to "descend from heaven with a shout, with the voice of an archangel, and with the trumpet of God. And the dead in Christ will rise first. Then we who are alive and remain shall be caught up together with them in the clouds to meet the Lord in the air. And thus we shall always be with the Lord" (1 Thessalonians

4:16, 17). From this we can determine that the Second Coming and the resurrection of Christians are simultaneous events.

Resurrection and Satan's Defeat

The conflict of the ages has pitted Satan against God, fighting over the control of mankind on this planet. If there were no resurrection of believers, then death would be the end and Satan would gain the ultimate victory. But we know that "Death is swallowed up in victory...through our Lord Jesus Christ" (1 Corinthians 15:54-57). As he resurrects believers from all ages to rule his coming kingdom, there will be everlasting proof of that victory.

How Are the Dead Raised?

It is intriguing to imagine dead bodies being brought back to life, but how in the world is it possible? How can decayed remnants be rejuvenated and reconstructed? After all, Humpty Dumpty was destined to remain in a million pieces, and the human body is infinitely more complex!

I remember speaking with a very distraught lady who had recently lost her husband. She was not troubled about his eternal destiny, because she knew his soul was with Christ in heaven. But she had just discovered a clause in her husband's will that required his body to be cremated and the ashes scattered over Lake Minnetonka just outside of Minneapolis. She was afraid he would miss out on the bodily resurrection because it would certainly be "impossible to find each of countless little ashes strewn across the bottom of the lake."

This rather bizarre dilemma was very real for that young widow. Fortunately, there was an extremely simple explanation with which to comfort her. First of all, with God *nothing* is impossible. Second, if God created the body, surely he can *re*-create it. Science tells us that matter changes form but never ceases to exist. Ice melts and becomes water, which evaporates and becomes vapor, which shows up as clouds, which dissolve into rain, which freezes and turns into ice, and on and on. Along the same line, as fire burns a log, the wood changes its composition and ceases to be wood, but its elements continue to exist in different forms—either as ashes on the ground or as vapor being absorbed into the atmosphere. God is well able to sort out all of these elements from wherever they may be in order to reconstruct the log. On the day of resurrection, he will collect all of the atoms that once comprised every dead believer and put together a new individual body which is like the original, but somehow perfected.

Paul used the example of a seed to describe our resurrection from death (1 Corinthians 15:35-44).

But someone will say, "How are the dead raised up? And with what body do they come?" Foolish one, what you sow is not made alive unless it dies. And what you sow, you do not sow that body that shall be, but mere grain—perhaps wheat or some other grain. But God gives it a body as it has pleased Him, and to each seed its own body. All flesh is not the same flesh, but there is one kind of flesh of men, another flesh of beasts, another of birds. There are also celestial bodies and terrestrial bodies; but the glory of the celestial is one, and the glory of the terrestrial is another. There is one glory of the sun, another glory of the moon, and another glory of the stars; for one star differs from another star in glory. So also is the resurrection of the dead. The body is sown in corruption, it is raised in incorruption. It is sown in dishonor, it is raised in glory. It is sown in weakness, it is raised in power. It is sown a natural body, it is raised a spiritual body. There is a natural body, and there is a spiritual body.

When a kernel of corn is placed into the ground, it has to die first before it can begin to grow. The same bundle of elements that went into the ground grows out of the ground, but now it turns into a stalk, ears, cobs, and many kernels of corn. The death of that first kernel resulted in its being transformed into an improved, expanded, glorified version of itself.

What Will Our New Bodies Look Like?
Paul told us that God will "transform our lowly body that it may be conformed to His glorious body . . ." (Philippians 3:21), so we

need only observe his resurrected body to learn what ours will be like.

Luke 24:36 gives a rather interesting picture that took place after his resurrection. The disciples were grieving in the upper room, the door being locked. "And as they said these things, Jesus Himself stood in the midst of them . . . ." The disciples were understandably startled, thinking they had seen a ghost. But Jesus immediately tried to calm them by showing them that He was, in fact, real. "Behold My hands and My feet, that it is I Myself. Handle Me and see, for a spirit does not have flesh and bones as you see I have" (v. 39). This must have been an incredible scene. Here stood Jesus in a physical, tangible body that was no longer subject to time and space, capable of entering a room without using the door!

An extraordinary feature of Christ's resurrection body probably startled the disciples: the absence of blood. Jesus referred to his body as "flesh and *bones,*" not "flesh and *blood.*" It is said that "life of all flesh is the blood" (Leviticus 17:14), but Jesus gave his life *and* his blood on Calvary's cross. His blood was "poured out for our sins," so he had none left. Scripture explains that flesh and blood shall not inhabit the kingdom of God.

Apparently we can expect to enjoy a good meal in our new bodies, because Jesus demonstrated that he was able to eat. "But while they still did not believe for joy, and marveled, He said to them, 'Have you any food here?' And they gave Him a piece of a broiled fish and some honeycomb. And He took it and ate in their presence" (Luke 24:41-43).

Like Jesus, we will be recognized in our new bodies. The disciples had no doubts about who appeared in their room. Even when he had prepared breakfast for them on the shore, "And none of the disciples dared ask Him, 'Who are You?'—Knowing that it was the Lord" (John 21:12).

In addition to recognizing people we have known, we will probably be able to recognize people we have never even met before. Remember the story of Lazarus and the rich man from the previous chapter? It is significant to note that the rich man knew that he was seeing Abraham, even though he lived hundreds of years before.

Resurrection and the Plan of God

When God created Adam and Eve, he intended for them to live forever and populate a race of people who would live forever. But Satan deceived Eve and introduced sin into the world, bringing death and destruction upon God's plan for man. That is why God sent his own son, Jesus Christ, so infinitely more valuable than all the men who have ever lived, to die in man's stead. By receiving him as a substitute for his sin and death, man can life forever and thus fulfill God's original plan. We are living today in the midst of this plan, which will be consummated when we are all resurrected to be eternally present with our Creator.

Logic Demands the Resurrection

If not for our resurrection unto eternal life, there is no justification for Jesus' coming to our world and his subsequent death on the cross. If man died like an animal and was never heard of again, there would be no need for God to make such a personal sacrifice. Since he did, we are forced to ask "Why?" The only explanation is that through his death, the damage of Adam and Eve's sin has been rectified, and man can yet enjoy the eternal blessings God originally intended for him. The resurrection is the means whereby man is once again able to fulfill his destiny.

Nowhere in Scripture, however, is there any suggestion that this destiny is necessarily favorable. Some will be "resurrected to everlasting life," others to "everlasting contempt." What makes the difference? Man's acceptance of Jesus Christ. Those who receive him will be raised to everlasting life; those who reject him will be raised to everlasting contempt. Since there are only two resurrections, and since you choose in this life whether or not you will accept Jesus Christ, ask yourself now in which resurrection you will take part.

CHAPTER FOUR

CHRISTIANS AFTER THE RESURRECTION

To Christians, the second coming of Jesus Christ is easily one of the most treasured teachings in the Bible. It is mentioned 318 times in the New Testament alone, making it one of the most prominent doctrines in Scripture, second only to the subject of salvation itself. What few Christians realize is that immediately after their "rapture" at the Lord's coming, they will stand before him at what is called the Judgment Seat of Christ.

The Christian who contemplates the wondrous afterlife which the Bible guarantees usually anticipates with joy his first personal meeting with Jesus Christ or the heaven he promised to prepare for his children. Few believers give much thought to the fact that their first activity will encompass their appearance at the Judgment Seat of Christ.

A look at the chart on page 31 clarifies that the rapture of the church and the resurrection of the human body for Christians are the same event, both located at the beginning of the tribulation. In 1 Corinthians 4:5 we are told that the Lord will judge us at his coming. That judgment is so awesome and significant that we shall examine it carefully. If the average Christian *really* understood that experience, it would no doubt encourage him to change his life style.

In his newly resurrected body, every believer will stand before his Lord to receive "the things done in his body, according to what he has done, whether it is good or bad" (2 Corinthians 5:10). There is probably no more important truth with which every Christian should be familiar than this, for it will determine his position of service during the millennium and may well affect his status in the eternal heaven which follows.

The most detailed passage of Scripture related to this coming event reads as follows:

For we are God's fellow workers; you are God's field, you are God's building. According to the grace of God which was given to me, as a wise master builder I have laid the foundation, and another builds on it. But let each one take heed how he builds on it. For no other foundation can anyone lay than that which is laid, which is Jesus Christ. Now if anyone builds on this foundation with gold, silver, precious stones, wood, hay, straw, each one's work will become manifest; for the Day will declare it, because it will be revealed by fire; and the fire will test each one's work, of what sort it is. If anyone's work which he has built on it endures, he will receive a reward. If anyone's work is burned, he will suffer loss; but he himself will be saved, yet so as through fire (1 Corinthians 3:9-15).

The chart on the next page depicts one artist's concept of that event.

By comparing the chart of 1 Corinthians 3:9-15 with the basic chart of this book found on page 31, you will find that this event takes place in the air, after the rapture, and *during the tribulation period*. It seems that Christians will face their Lord in judgment while the unsaved living world goes through the awful holocaust that yet awaits it: the seven year tribulation period noted on the main timeline of the chart. This will provide ample time to prepare all believers to receive their rewards and establish their positions to rule and reign with Christ when he comes to set up his millennial kingdom. This will be covered in detail in the next chapter.

JUDGMENT OF THE BELIEVERS

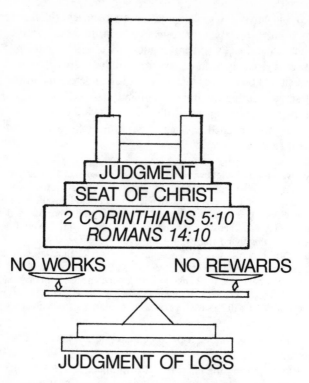

JUDGMENT
SEAT OF CHRIST
2 CORINTHIANS 5:10
ROMANS 14:10

NO WORKS   NO REWARDS

JUDGMENT OF LOSS

PRECIOUS STONES   CROWN OF LIFE

JUDGMENT OF REWARD
1 CORINTHIANS 3:14

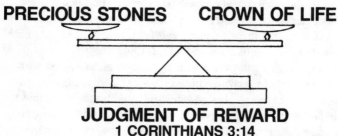

GOOD WORKS

1. QUALITY
   Matthew 25:14-30
2. QUANTITY
   Luke 19:11-27

BAD WORKS

1. GOOD WORKS DONE
   WITH EVIL MOTIVE
2. HIDDEN COUNSELS
3. UNCONFESSED SIN

2 JOHN 8

"The foundation which no man can lay" is obviously salvation independent of good works. For instance, a Sunday school teacher from a liberal church received Christ one Sunday evening. Later, after hearing a message on the Judgment Seat of Christ, she asked, "Will I receive any rewards for the nine years I taught Sunday school in that liberal church?" I answered, "No, that was like throwing good things into quicksand—they were swallowed up because you had no foundation." No one can accumulate good works until he has accepted salvation through Christ. After that foundation is laid, he can build on it "gold, silver, precious stones, wood, hay, or straw."

As mentioned in 2 Corinthians 5:10, the Judgment Seat of Christ is to determine the quality of our works, "good or bad." The wood, hay, and straw works are "good works" that merely simulate the real thing. They will be destroyed in the fire intended to "try every man's work." But before we get to that, we had better examine what the Bible means by "good works."

What Is a "Good Work"?

Since good works bring extraordinary rewards, we need to know what constitutes a "good work." The following are some possibilities described in Scripture.

Witness. One type of good work is mentioned in Matthew 5:16: "Let your light so shine before men, that they may see your good works and glorify your Father who is in heaven." A Christian is expected to let his light shine for the world to see. He represents the Lord Jesus Christ to a world that, for the most part, does not know him. Part of a Christian's good works involves living a pure life and being a consistent witness for the Lord.

Worship. Jesus referred to worship of himself as a good work. When a woman anointed his head with precious ointment, he told his anxious disciples to leave her alone because she had "done a good work for Me" (Matthew 26:7-10). Very often we limit our concept of worship to adoration of and praise to God. But he likewise considers it "a good work" that will be included at the Judgment Seat.

Generosity. In 1 Timothy 6:18 we learn that being "rich" in good works involves being generous and willing to share. It is interesting that the verse says "*ready* to give" and "willing to share." In other words, it is primarily the *attitude* of generosity that comprises the good work. True, we are expected to follow through if called upon to demonstrate our intentions, but as we shall see later, wrong motivations can take the "good" out of "good works." If we give grudgingly or share the gospel because we're afraid we will be punished if we don't, that is not being rich in good works. But all acts performed with proper motives will stand the test of fire and receive a reward.

Jesus made it clear that nothing is too small to be considered a good work. Recorded in Matthew 10:42 is the statement, "And whoever gives one of these little ones only a cup of cold water in the name of a disciple, assuredly, I say to you, he will by no means lose his reward." Even the most apparently insignificant word or deed done for the glory of the Lord will receive divine compensation.

It is safe to conclude from the above that almost anything a Christian does for Jesus Christ after he is born-again will earn a reward. This would include the numerous formal acts of service in his local church such as teaching Sunday school, singing in the choir, ushering, serving on boards and committees, directing a bus ministry, participating in evangelism, and witnessing to his friends. I have long been convinced that many of the unsung heroes of the church will be rewarded for deeds that have gone almost entirely unnoticed. Such acts would include remembering neighbors in their hour of suffering, comforting the bereaved and the handicapped, caring for infants, adopting or housing homeless children, or engaging in morally significant civic or political activities. Even the holding of a so-called "political office" can have an impact when done for Jesus Christ and will be worthy of a reward. I know a man who serves on a college board of trustees. Many of the proceedings sicken his heart, but he knows that if he were not involved, his replacement would most likely be a humanist.

In this day of humanistically inspired depravity in many of our public schools, it is most difficult to stand for Christ and serve as a moral influence. Some of the unrecognized heroes in that day of judgment will be dedicated Christian school teachers who have withstood the erosion of morality and the high pressures of SIECUS sex education and its humanistic philosophy. I know several Christians who have volunteered to teach sex education in their schools merely because they wanted to do something for Christ and to advance the cause of moral decency in his name. The God who spared Nineveh for the 60,000 children who did not know the difference between their right hand and their left will no doubt look with special favor upon those who have borne personal and professional insult or anguish for the sake of today's children.

These are only some of the hundreds of illustrations that could be used concerning Christians who will be awarded good works in that day of judgment.

The Formula for Rewards

While it is impossible to list all of the specific illustrations of reward-producing activities in life, we can offer some basic guidelines. We will then return to the fire test as shown on our chart (page 54) to indicate how they relate to eternal rewards. In many parables, our Lord spoke of a householder or a king who went on a long journey and returned to his servants, demanding an accounting of what they had done in his absence. This is much like our Lord's departure into heaven two thousand years ago with the promise that he would return one day, demanding an accounting of mankind. The believer's profit-and-loss statement will not determine whether he is saved or lost—that was already assured by his acceptance of Christ—but it will specify the degree of his reward.

Three parables are particularly appropriate to the judgment of Christians. We shall see that the formula for rewards will involve quantity, quality, and time.

Quantity

In Luke 19:11-27, Jesus indicates that he expects a quantity return for what he has entrusted to us. A nobleman gave each of his servants one pound to invest while he was out of the country. When he came back and found that one servant had earned ten more, he was very pleased and made him "ruler over ten cities." Another servant had gained five more pounds and was given charge of "five cities." The rewards granted these servants were directly proportionate to the increase they had earned from their original pound. Applying this principle to good works, it simply means that our rewards will be proportionate to the degree that we have used our God-given opportunities to serve him and one another. God does expect results from our lives.

Quality

Still another aspect of good works will be measured at the judgment: quality. How much did we actually accomplish by our good works in relation to the talents we inherited in the first place?

Remember the parable of the talents? (See Matthew 25:14-30.) The master gave five talents to one of his servants and two talents to another—"each according to his own ability." The five-talent man earned five more and the two-talent man two more. Notice that both of them received the same reward, for he said, "Well done, good and faithful servant; you have been faithful over a few things, I will make you ruler over many things." The two-talent man who doubled his talents did not receive less than the five-talent man who doubled his. (The important thing is they both doubled what they had started out with.) God doesn't compare our good works with anyone else's. Since he knows what talents, abilities, and opportunities we have at our disposal, we will be accountable only for them.

I often meet Christians who are enormously talented but do little or nothing for Jesus Christ. How I wish I could get them to understand that "to whom much is given, much will be required in the day of judgment." Unfortunately, many of the most talented Christians seem to waste their talents on the god of this world or ephemeral items that will soon be burned up, neglecting to invest their creativity in the things of Jesus Christ.

On the other hand, I meet Christians who possess very meager talents and refuse to use even those, calling themselves "no-talent Christians." Frankly, the closest I have ever encountered to an untalented Christian was one who had the excuse of being mentally retarded. And even then, God can use a heart of pure motivation.

Dr. George W. Truett tells the charming story of a great surgeon who attended his church with his Christian wife but was himself an unbeliever. Many in the congregation prayed for the man's salvation. One Sunday morning, as Dr. Truett was preaching a strong evangelistic message, he was deeply moved about the man's salvation. During the invitation he saw a twelve-year-old mentally retarded girl slip over to the famous doctor, tug on his coat, and speak to him. Not realizing that she had been the physician's patient, Dr. Truett reports that he groaned in his spirit, wondering if this girl had interfered with the work of the Holy Spirit. During the last stanza of the invitation the doctor moved out of his pew and walked down to receive Christ. Afterward Dr. Truett asked what it was in his message that had moved him to come to Christ. "It was not your sermon, Dr. Truett; it was the little girl's comment." She had simply asked, "Doctor, do you want to go to heaven?" He had replied, "No." So she quickly responded, "Then you'll just have to go to hell." Yes, even a retarded twelve-year-old can be used by the Spirit of God if she is available to him. Never underestimate meager talents when empowered by the Holy Spirit.

Time

Believers are expected to give faithful service for as long as they are employed by the Master. Someone newly saved (like the thief on the cross next to Christ) has little time to exercise his talents, but a Christian of forty years will have to show how well he used that time to serve the Lord.

Christians in increasing number are being unduly influenced by today's ideas of how to spend leisure time and retirement. As a pastor I have observed that in the past Christians used the passage of their teenage children from the home into marriage or college as an impetus to greater heights of Christian activity. Now such parents are instead becoming self-indulgent. Many go overboard with recreation, pet hobbies, or other activities rather than investing themselves in the work of the kingdom of God. This they do to their own peril on judgment day, for God holds us accountable to serve him as long as we have breath.

In Matthew 20:1-16 our Lord told the story of the landowner who hired individuals for a day's work, promising to pay them the going rate of a penny (probably equivalent to thirty or forty dollars today). Later in the day he hired additional men and promised to pay them whatever was right. Later he hired even more help. At the end of the day, though he incurred the wrath of those who had worked the longest, he paid all of his employees a day's wage for their work. Likewise, Christians will be held accountable to serve the Lord for as many years as he gives them after their conversion. Every child of God is challenged to be faithful unto death in serving his Lord (Revelation 2:10).

A helpful formula that summarizes our discussion on judgment and rewards for good works may be stated as follows:

QUANTITY + QUALITY   + FAITHFUL   = REWARD
                                    SERVICE

POUNDS   + TALENTS   + TIME   = REWARD
Luke 19:11-27   *Matthew*   *Matthew*
                    25:14-30   *20:1-16*

Bad Works

The above formula presupposes that good works were performed with a good motive. Now we come to bad works, which are evidently those that will be burned when tested by fire and revealed to be nothing more than wood, hay, and straw. Bad works fall into three categories: good works enacted with an evil motive, "hidden counsels of the heart" that are contrary to God's will, and unconfessed sin.

Good Works—Bad Motives

Jesus tells us time and again that deeds initiated with the intention of impressing men are virtually worthless in his sight. In Matthew 6:2 he states flatly that anyone who does a good work in order to receive praise from others will receive no reward from God. The earthly approval he was seeking is the total reward he will receive. Ephesians 6:7 tells us that we should render our service to the Lord, not to men. Colossians 3:23 directs us to work for Christ, discharging our duties as unto the Lord and not unto men.

This will probably be the most tragic part of the judgment of fire for some believers' works. Many accomplishments considered to be good works in this life will be revealed as having self-serving motives behind them. Christian service done for any other purpose than the glory and honor of Jesus Christ will be exposed as wood, hay, and straw and will be consumed by fire.

On a regular basis every Christian should forthrightly ask himself, "Why do I do what I'm doing?" If you sing in the choir, you can well ask if you are singing to be seen of men or to magnify Jesus Christ. If you are a soloist, what is your motivation? To stand up before the congregation and impress them with your vocal expertise—or to sing to the glory of God? It is readily apparent from this concept that two singers can participate in a duet, spending the same amount of preparation and performance time, but only one may receive a reward because only one did it as unto the Lord. The same can be applied to Christian service in church offices and every other work for Christ. I wonder if much of the strife and

JUDGMENT OF REWARD

CROWN OF
REJOICING
1 THESSALONIANS 2:19, 20

CROWN OF GLORY
1 PETER 5:4

INCORRUPTIBLE
CROWN
1 CORINTHIANS 9:25

CROWN OF
RIGHTEOUSNESS
2 TIMOTHY 4:8

PRECIOUS STONES   CROWN OF LIFE
REVELATION 2:10

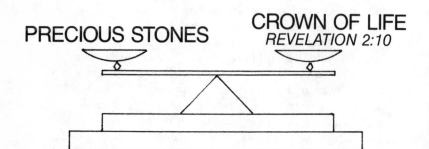

1 CORINTHIANS 3:14
"WELL DONE, THOU GOOD
AND FAITHFUL SERVANT"

bitterness engendered in some churches and Christian groups could be avoided if more of the activities were done to the glory of God.

Hidden Counsels

In 1 Corinthians 4:5 it states that at this judgment Christ will "make manifest the counsels of the hearts." All of the secret sins and evil thoughts we believe to be thoroughly buried in our hearts will be brought to the surface and revealed under the bright searchlight of Christ's judgment. These hidden counsels, similar to the bad motives mentioned above, are known only to God. Unquestionably, many good Christian works have been negated by improper hidden motives and thoughts. Some engage in Christian activities while indulging in impure, angry, or revengeful thought patterns. Such mental sins will be revealed at the judgment, causing the destruction of what would otherwise have been good works. God wants to use your "vessel," but he insists that it be clean.

Unconfessed Sin

We are told in 1 John 1:9, "If we confess our sins, He is faithful and just to forgive us our sins and to cleanse us from all unrighteousness." It is very comforting to know that if we Christians just confess our sins, they are immediately forgiven. But what if we *don't*? A confessed sin is forgotten in the eyes of God and "remembered against us no more," but if we refuse to confess and turn from our sin, we will be confronted with it at Christ's judgment seat. Once again, keep in mind that it is possible to lose good works ("Look to yourselves, that we not lose those things we have worked for, but that we receive a full reward" 2 John 8). I believe that if we are brought before Jesus Christ with unconfessed sin in our lives, we will have to pay for that sin by the loss of good works already laid up in heaven.

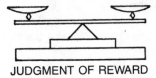

JUDGMENT OF REWARD

1 Corinthians 3:14: "If anyone's work which he has built on it endures, he will receive a reward."

Occasionally I meet Christians who object to serving Christ for rewards in heaven. I can certainly understand their feeling, because our motivation for faithful service should only be love for him. However, Jesus himself challenged us, "But lay up for yourselves treasures in heaven, where neither moth nor rust destroys and where thieves do not break in and steal" (Matthew 6:20). In addition, Hebrews 11:25, 26 indicates that Moses turned his back on the treasures of Egypt because he considered the reproach of Christ "greater riches . . .for he looked to the reward." This would indicate dual motivations; (1) a genuine love for God prompted him to give his life in service to leading the children of Israel out of Egypt, and (2) eternal rewards were valued much more highly than honorariums. And after 4,000 years, who can deny that Moses was right? Many other faithful servants of Christ have turned their backs on profitable ventures or vocations because they preferred to invest themselves in the eternal works of God. Naturally, such individuals will receive an everlasting reward.

The Purpose

Throughout the Word of God, gold has been used as a symbol of the deity and glory of the Lord. Silver is a type of redemption. In the Old Testament, Israel always paid their redemption money in silver, according to the specific command of God. Malachi 3:17 says, "And they shall be mine, saith the Lord of hosts, in that day when I make up my jewels." This verse indicates that to God the Father, souls are metaphorically looked upon as jewels. On that basis, the symbols used by the Lord Jesus for "good works" (gold, silver and precious stones) would indicate the possibility of the gold representing those things which we have done to glorify Christ. The silver will depict our endeavors to spread the story of his redemption, such as Sunday school teaching, writing letters, or utilizing any other witnessing tool available to the child of God. The precious stones will symbolize the deeds of those souls whom we have had the joy of leading out of darkness into everlasting light (see Daniel 12:3).

The two greatest enemies of Christian service, selfishness and laziness, have robbed many of God's children of rewards they should have received. Don't let these enemies overcome you lest you become a victim of the *judgment of loss* (1 Corinthians 3:15).

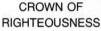
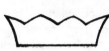

CROWN OF RIGHTEOUSNESS

2 Timothy 4:8: "Finally, there is laid up for me the crown of righteousness, which the Lord, the righteous Judge, will give me on that Day; and not to me only, but also to all who have loved His appearing."

A special crown is reserved for those Christians who, inspired by the imminent return of Christ, have lived a very righteous and holy life. God does not demand talented vessels for his service. In fact, we need to remember that what comes from our lives is accomplished by his power, not our skills or talent. He simply lays down one major requirement: that a Christian be clean. Somehow the doctrine of the imminent return of Christ has a purifying effect upon the believer (see Titus 2:12-14 and 1 John 3:2, 3).

INCORRUPTIBLE CROWN

1 Corinthians 9:25-27: "And everyone who competes for the prize is temperate in all things. Now they do it to obtain a perishable crown, but we an imperishable. Therefore I run thus: not with uncertainty. Thus I fight: not as one who beats the air. But I discipline my body and bring it into subjection, lest, when I have preached to others, I myself should become disqualified."

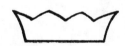

This crown often called the "victor's crown," is conferred upon those who "keep under their body and bring it into subjection." That is, those who have purged themselves from the inducements and pleasures of the world in order to be of profitable service for the Lord Jesus Christ merit this crown. Many a child of God has relinquished a lifelong enjoyment so that he could more readily and efficiently serve Christ.

I once knew a Christian who sold his cottage at the lake, not because there was anything wrong with it, but because he decided that he was spending too many of his weekends at the lake and as a result was neglecting his service for Christ. The victor's crown is one that the worldly, self-appeasing, self-indulgent Christian will not receive. It is reserved for those who have paid the price to run the race of Christian service victoriously.

One evening, in the home of a couple in our church, I had the opportunity to meet two world-famous track stars; one had broken the four-minute mile, the other had won the 10,000 meter Olympic race in Japan. Neither athlete would have been successful if he had permitted himself the same sedentary life style as the average American. If they had eaten the same junk food and sugar-infested goodies as their peers, they would never have distinguished themselves on the running track. So it is in the Christian's life. Many a clean, holy-living Christian passes up the potential of earned rewards because he is unwilling to adopt the extra responsibility of teaching a Sunday school class regularly or going out Monday night witnessing instead of enjoying weekend jaunts or watching NFL football. He will not extend himself in service that will earn the incorruptible crown.

CROWN OF LIFE

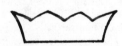

James 1:12: "Blessed is the man who endures temptation; for when he has been proved, he will receive the crown of life which the Lord has promised to those who love Him."

This crown is often called the "martyr's crown" or the sufferer's crown—one which will rectify the many injustices suffered in life, even among Christians whose pathway through life is pleasant and enjoyable. Whether they live a victorious, aggressive Christian life or not seems to make little difference. It appears that everything they touch turns to gold.

On the other hand, you have known Christians who have suffered much. Some have been tried incessantly. It seems that for them, everything goes wrong, and yet through it all they have manifested a sweet Christian spirit. To these will be given the "crown of life." The crown is also a special reward for those who have been "faithful unto death" as a witness for Christ (Revelation 2:10).

Shortly after the tragedy that claimed the lives of five missionaries at the hand of the Auca Indians in Ecuador, I heard several friends exclaim that these young men had "lost their lives." That is not true! In reality they *gave* their lives—and in so doing earned for themselves the crown of life that is forever.

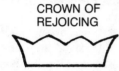

CROWN OF REJOICING

1 Thessalonians 2:19: "For what is our hope, or joy, or crown of rejoicing? Is it not even you in the presence of our Lord Jesus Christ at His coming?"

This is often referred to as the "soul winner's" crown. This special crown is reserved for those who have devoted their primary attention to the salvation of lost souls. Often this service is rendered obscurely, unknown to other Christians. We in the Christian church often exalt and laud those who are "well appearing" but nevertheless fruitless Christians. This injustice will be rectified by God; those who have been true soul-winners will receive the "crown of rejoicing." Some of the unsung heroes of the church and in Christian circles who have given themselves emphatically to winning people to Christ will rejoice in that day that they denied themselves and expended their energies upon soul-winning.

CROWN OF GLORY

1 Peter 5:1, 4: "The elders who are among you I exhort, I who am a fellow elder and a witness of the sufferings of Christ, and also a partaker of the glory that will be revealed: and when the Chief Shepherd appears, you will receive the crown of glory that does not fade away."

This is often called the "shepherd's crown" or the pastor's crown. It is reserved for those who have given their lives to the teaching of the Word of God. This crown should be an incentive to every young person who is considering how to invest his life. In what endeavor could one invest his life with greater return than teaching the Word of God?

Personally, I am inclined to feel that this crown will also be won by faithful Sunday school teachers. Although their flock may not be as large as the pastor's, nevertheless they are "feeding the flock"—obviously a reference to teaching the Word of God to the Lord's sheep. Usually we think of this in relation to pastor-teachers, and certainly it includes them, but I believe it also encompasses Sunday school teachers who are instructing elders in the average church. If I were a layman, knowing what I know about the joys of expounding the Word of God and the elder's crown, I would ask God to make me a Bible teacher. It is fulfilling in this life and rewarding in the life to come.

I have observed in all service for Christ one fundamental rule: "He that is faithful in few things will he make ruler over many" (Matthew 25:23). I have known individuals refuse to do anything at all because they couldn't embark upon a major enterprise first. But I have never seen a person begin at the top in Christian service. Instead, everyone must start out small and prove himself faithful before God will provide him greater opportunities. It is my privilege to know many of the outstanding Bible teachers and ministers in the country today, and they all can trace their early days of service to faithfully proclaiming the Word of God to a handful of people. Had they not proven faithful in those "small things," they would not enjoy their present situations.

Married Partners Sharing Rewards

Solomon said, "An excellent wife is the crown of her husband, but she who shames him is as rottenness to his bones." Having pastored in a city that seldom harbors less than 100,000 Navy personnel, I have enjoyed friendships with many chaplains and their wives through the years. These officers go out to sea for long periods of time, winning men to Christ and training them in the Word, while their wives remain at home, tending the children and keeping the home stable. Many times I have mused that at the Judgment Seat of Christ, these faithful wives will share their husbands' rewards. The chaplain could not be a faithful servant of God if he did not have a faithful wife, and this can be said for every missionary, minister, or other servant of God. This principle appeared in David's classic statement to the soldiers who stayed behind by the baggage: "We share and share alike—those who go to battle and those who guard the equipment" (1 Samuel 30:24, TLB).

Purpose of the Crowns

Crowns are a symbol of authority: As such, they denote the authority that will be granted to Christians during the millennial period when we reign with Christ for a thousand years. Obviously, Christians will not be running around with one or more crowns upon their heads any more than the Queen of England wears a crown all the time. The fact that she is the queen entitles her to wear the crown, which gives her the authority to exercise her queenly prerogatives.

So it will be with believers during the millennium. Christians are now earning their position of service for Christ during the millennium. Our most enjoyable and profitable activities on this earth involve service for Jesus Christ. In like manner our most exciting experiences in the millennial kingdom will include administration of his program. If Christians really understood this, they would surely be motivated to pursue better and more lasting heights of Christian service.

Crowns Can Be Lost

Revelation 3:11: "Behold I come quickly! Hold fast what you have, that no one take your crown."

The above verse is another reminder (along with 2 John 8) that it is possible to "lose those things we have worked for" by unfaithful service. Many a Christian has served the Lord for many years, then has capitulated to the enticement of carnality, sensuality, or some other temptation which has turned him from serving Christ to reveling in the appetites of the flesh. Although such individuals will be saved when they die, they will forfeit their reward. In some cases, they will lose the crowns which they have already earned. Every Christian who desires to serve Christ to the maximum during the millennium is advised to heed our Lord's challenge to the church of Smyrna in Revelation 2:10, "Be faithful until death, and I will give you the crown of life."

Positional Rewards

1 Peter 1:6, 7: "In this you greatly rejoice, though now for a little while, if need be, you have been grieved by manifold temptations, that the genuineness of your faith, being much more precious than gold that perishes, though it is tested with fire, may be found to praise, honor, and glory at the revelation of Jesus Christ."

In addition to the crown rewards, there are also positional rewards listed by the apostle Peter as praise, honor, and glory.

1. EVERY MAN SHALL RECEIVE PRAISE

"In the name of our Lord Jesus Christ, when you are gathered together, along with my spirit, with the power of our Lord Jesus Christ" (1 Corinthians 5:4).

2. THOSE WHO SERVE CHRIST WILL BE HONORED

"If anyone serves me, let him follow Me; and where I am, there My servant will be also. If anyone serves Me, him My Father will honor" (John 12:26).

3. SUFFERERS WILL BE GLORIFIED

"Beloved, do not think it strange concerning the fiery trial which is to try you, as though some strange thing happened to you; but rejoice, insofar as you are partakers of Christ's sufferings, that when His glory is revealed, you may also be glad with exceeding joy. If you are reproached for the name of Christ, blessed are you, for the Spirit of glory and of God rests on you. On their part He is blasphemed, but on your part He is glorified" (1 Peter 4:12-14).

Comparing these three texts, we find that everyone will receive praise at the judgment seat. This is the minimal reward. In addition, those who *serve Christ* will be honored. Christians living in an age of grace should understand that although salvation is free because of the grace of God, works are the result of self-denial, consecration, and effort on the part of the believer. Then, in some way, those who have suffered most for Christ will receive special glory from him. This is certainly in accord with the just nature of God, who plans to reward every man according to his works. I think we are all going to be surprised when we stand before the great Judge to find that many of the least known Christians in this life who have humbly served their Lord will be elevated to a greater position and reward than some of the "elite." The Bible teaches that we reap what we sow. This life serves as the planting time; the future life brings harvest. Just as a farmer must toil to plant his seed in the spring in order to harvest in the fall, so we as Christians have to pay the price of service for Christ now in order to receive our rewards in eternity and hear our Master say, "Well done, good and faithful servant. Enter into the joy of your master."

Years ago I heard a great Bible teacher, M. R. DeHaan, say, "To come to Christ costs you nothing, to follow Christ costs you something, to serve Christ will cost you everything."

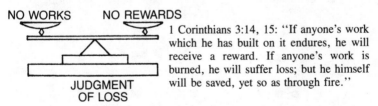

1 Corinthians 3:14, 15: "If anyone's work which he has built on it endures, he will receive a reward. If anyone's work is burned, he will suffer loss; but he himself will be saved, yet so as through fire."

This discussion of reward is not complete until we examine the tragedy which appears in the above verses. Many Christians whose carnal appetites and refusal to crucify the old man have kept them from working for their Lord will receive absolutely no reward at the Judgment Seat of Christ. It is obvious from these verses that salvation is not jeopardized, for he is saved "so as through fire." The idiom "as through fire" is similar to our contemporary adage, "saved by the skin of his teeth." Many a Christian will be saved, but with absolutely nothing to show for his life of Christian service.

When I pastored in Minneapolis, a tragedy occurred one night which involved a newly divorced woman who was pleased that she had been decreed "everything": their beautiful four-year-old child, their ranch style house, and the new car in the garage. Her husband retained little of their property and was saddled with alimony and with house and car payments. That night she was awakened by firemen warning her that the house was on fire. Within thirty minutes it had burned to the ground. She lost everything, including the life of her precious child. As she stood in the snow watching her worldly possessions go up in smoke, she acquired a painful insight into what it means to be "saved so as through fire."

The only difference between that woman's experience and that of Christians on judgment day is that she was young enough to start over. At the Judgment Seat of Christ, our opportunities to earn rewards will be over. We have only one life to give in service for Christ, but we must offer it now.

CHAPTER FIVE

ONE THOUSAND YEARS OF PEACE

Man's fascination for the future finds its greatest satisfaction in the coming kingdom of peace described in literally hundreds of passages in the Bible. Many names are assigned to it, such as the Kingdom Age, the Millennium, the Age of Peace, the Reign of Christ. The best known is simply the Kingdom.

This coming kingdom should not be confused with "heaven." Even though there are many similarities, heaven will contain all the good things of the millennium kingdom plus many more—and it is eternal. The Kingdom Age is temporary, for it lasts only 1,000 years.

The Kingdom Age will usher in the utopian kind of peace for which every normal human being has yearned. Since the beginning of time, man has demonstrated hatred toward his fellow man and his natural tendencies for greed through unnecessary wars. Even as I write this, set before me is an issue of *U. S. News and World Report* showing a map of the world with twenty-three "hot spots," men killing their fellow countrymen (and this is happening thirty-five years after the establishment of the United Nations, which was supposed to provide the world a means for discontinuing war.) As long as Satan is roaming free on this earth, there will always be wars. He is not only a deceiver of men, but he literally hates men and throughout history has pitted one nation against the other. But there shall come a time when he is bound in the bottomless pit, ushering in the Kingdom Age of peace.

Although there are so many biblical references to the Kingdom Age, most Christians know very little about this delightful period in which they will rule and reign with Christ for a thousand years.

The Kingdom in the Old Testament

Belief in the Kingdom Age is one teaching shared by both Jews and Christians. Throughout the Old Testament, Israel was promised the return of the kingdom of David, to be ruled by their Messiah. But this is where the similarities cease, for the Jews believe that the Messiah will come in the future, whereas Christians believe he came already and will come again. The Jews failed to recognize two kinds of prophecies concerning the advent of the Messiah. The first had to do with his coming to suffer for the sins of mankind, as described in Isaiah 53. The second phase relates to his coming in power and great glory to reign. It is impossible to list all of the Old Testament passages that predicted the kingdom, but we shall highlight three of them.

Isaiah 9:6, 7
For unto us a child is born, unto us a son is given: and the government shall be upon his shoulder: and his name shall be called Wonderful, Counsellor, The mighty God, The everlasting Father, The Prince of Peace. Of the increase of his government and peace there shall be no end, upon the throne of David, and upon his kingdom, to order it, and to establish it with judgment and with justice from henceforth even for ever. The zeal of the Lord of hosts will perform this.

That this prophecy was not completely fulfilled at the time of our Lord's first coming is obvious. At no time was the government upon Jesus' shoulder, nor has the world enjoyed the kingdom of righteousness and justice it describes. This kingdom will be established by our Lord when he comes again.

Daniel 2:31-35
Thou, O king, sawest, and behold a great image. This great image, whose brightness was excellent, stood before thee; and the form thereof was terrible. This image's head was of fine gold, his breast and his arms of silver, his belly and his thighs of brass, his legs of iron, his feet part of iron and part of clay. Thou sawest till that a stone was cut out without hands, which smote the image upon his feet that were of iron and clay, and brake them to pieces. Then was the iron, the clay, the brass, the silver, and the gold, broken to pieces together, and became like the chaff of the summer threshingfloors; and the wind carried them away, that no place was found for them: and the stone that smote the image became a great mountain, and filled the whole earth.

Daniel 2:44, 45 (Interpretation)
And in the days of these kings shall the God of heaven set up a kingdom, which shall never be destroyed: and the kingdom shall not be left to other people; but it shall break in pieces and consume all these kingdoms, and it shall stand for ever. Forasmuch as thou sawest that the stone was cut out of the mountain without hands, and that it brake in pieces the iron, the brass, the clay, the silver, and the gold; the great God hath made known to the king what shall come to pass hereafter: and the dream is certain, and the interpretation thereof sure.

Nebuchadnezzar, the king of Babylon and first world emperor, had a dream that troubled him, but he could not remember it, despite the assistance of soothsayers and astrologers. When Daniel, the captive Hebrew prince, was summoned, through the power of God he recalled and interpreted the dream. Most Bible scholars believe that Daniel 2 is a basic preview of world history, predicting the coming Kingdom Age after four successive world-wide kingdoms. Nebuchadnezzar and his Babylonian empire were represented as the head of gold. Then came the Medo-Persians represented by the arms and chest of silver, followed by the belly and thighs of brass, which coincided with the Greek empire. The two legs symbolized the Roman empire, which was later divided into eastern and western empires.

The most fascinating aspect of this description is that a stone cut without hands struck the image, ground it to powder, and became a mountain that filled the whole earth. This symbolic prophecy is easily interpreted by Bible scholars who recognize that Christ is the rock upon which the church has been built. It was the rock that followed Israel during their Old Testament wanderings, through the wilderness, providing their need for water (1 Corinthians 10:4). The fact that the rock cut without human hands grinds the governmental kingdoms of the world to powder means that it will destroy man's attempts at government, and replace them with God's theocratic reign, which will fill the whole earth.

Man's romance with government, particularly worldwide government, certainly didn't start with the United Nations' dream, consummated in 1945. And man's degenerated heart will never produce an era of peace. The United Nations itself is an evidence of that fact. This worldwide organization was purportedly founded to usher in world peace, but it must face the historical reality that there have been more wars in its thirty-five-year history than in any comparable period of the world's history.

Surprisingly enough, I agree with one area of thinking on the part of the United Nations' advocates: that the only hope for world peace is a one-world dictator. However, we disagree on the qualifications of that dictator. Competent Bible scholars concur that no mere human being is competent to fill such a position. History proves that power corrupts, and absolute power corrupts absolutely. Therefore, if a *man* were given that role, we would eventually discover a world filled with slaves. The earth desperately needs a holy, loving, merciful dictator who will treat mankind equitably. Jesus Christ alone qualifies for that role, and until he comes, this world will never know peace.

An interesting sidelight of the prophecy is that through Daniel, God predicted that there would only be four worldwide empires until Christ comes. Historically that has been true. In fact, if one of the many would-be world dictators—Genghis Khan, Napoleon, Kaiser Wilhelm, Adolf Hitler, or Joseph Stalin—had succeeded, they would have destroyed the reliability of the Bible. Such, however, was not the case, and there will not be another world empire until the kingdom of Jesus Christ fills the entire earth.

Scores of other Old Testament passages could be used to show the anticipation of the Jews for that special kingdom of God. We will use some of these as we describe the conditions of the kingdom age.

The Kingdom in the New Testament

Most Christians are familiar with our Lord's instruction that we pray: "Your kingdom come, your will be done, on earth as it is in heaven." We have been offering that prayer for almost two thousand years. It has not been fulfilled, not because God is disinterested, but because God's prophetic calendar has not been fulfilled. However, those conversant with the twelve basic signs of the end of the age realize that we are rapidly approaching the time of that kingdom.

Matthew 13 contains one of the most significant teachings of our Lord regarding the kingdom of heaven. He launched this kingdom spiritually during his first coming but promised to consummate it with his second coming.

Several of the parables reviewed earlier in this book contain references to a householder or king or lord who journeyed into a far country and returned to demand an accounting. These parables depict life during the Church Age that culminates in the return of Christ to the earth. The parable of the talents in Matthew 25:14-30 is a good example.

The People of the Kingdom

"When the Son of Man comes in His glory, and all the holy angels with Him, then He will sit on the throne of His glory. And all the nations will be gathered before Him, and He will separate them one from another, as a shepherd divides his sheep from the goats. And He will set the sheep on His right hand, but the goats on the left. Then the King will say to those on His right hand, 'Come, you blessed of My Father, inherit the kingdom prepared for you from the foundation of the world: for I was hungry and you gave Me food; I was thirsty and you gave Me drink; I was a stranger and you took Me in; I was naked and you clothed Me; I was sick and you visited Me; I was in prison and you came to Me.' Then the righteous will answer Him, saying, 'Lord, when did we see You hungry and feed You, or thirsty and give You drink? When did we see You a stranger and take You in, or naked and clothe You? Or when did we see You sick, or in prison, and come to see You?' And the King will answer and say to them, 'Assuredly, I say to you, inasmuch as you have done it to one of the least of these My brethren, you have done it to Me.' Then He will also say to those on the left hand, 'Depart from Me, you cursed, into the everlasting fire prepared for the devil and his angels: for I was hungry and you gave Me no food; I was thirsty and you gave Me no drink; I was a stranger and you did not take Me in, naked and you did not clothe Me, sick and in prison and you did not visit Me.' Then they will also answer Him, saying, 'Lord, when did we see You hungry or thirsty or a stranger or naked or sick or in prison, and did not minister to You?' Then He will answer them, saying, 'Assuredly, I say to you, inasmuch as you did not do it to one of the least of these, you did not do it to Me.' And these will go away into everlasting punishment, but the righteous into eternal life" (Matthew 25:31-46).

Who will enter the Kingdom Age? It has been promised to the Jews and to the Christians but forbidden to those who "would offend" (which obviously refers to unbelievers). To rightly understand the occupants of the kingdom, we must read Matthew 25:31-46.

This parable, a genuine prophecy of our Lord, is one of the most incredible teachings in the Bible. It contains something taught nowhere else. This is the only passage in which people are offered entrance into the kingdom of God by good works. Since Ephesians 2:8, 9 and many other sections of Scripture make it clear that salvation is not conferred because of works, but is the free gift of God, we must conclude that inheriting an entrance into the kingdom and receiving salvation are not one and the same.

This passage is often called "the judgment of the nations," for it follows the tribulation period when antichrist will have persecuted the Jews and Christians for three and a half years because of his humanistically inspired antagonism to God. Most people may not be aware of the fact that humanism is basically the religion of the antichrist. That is why we find modern humanism has one passionate hatred: Christianity and its morality, decency, integrity, etc.

When Christ comes, as described in Revelation 19, there will only be four kinds of people on the earth:

1. Millions of unsaved followers who have taken the mark of the beast.

2. Individuals who refused to take the mark of the antichrist (or lived in outlying areas where his troops had not as yet reached) and who befriended the Jews during their time of persecution.

3. A few Christians who will be raptured just before Christ comes to the earth, so that the entire body of Christ will go into the millennium in their resurrected bodies (see Psalm 6:1-6); these have not been massacred during the tribulation because of their refusal to take the mark of the beast (Revelation 7:3, 4).

4. The Jews who have not been killed by the antichrist because they were befriended by the "sheep."

Since the Lord will destroy the unsaved because of their rejection of him and their acceptance of antichrist, only two kinds of people living natural lives will populate the millennium at its inception. They will be the Jews and their Gentile protectors during the last three and a half years. This may indicate that instead of the great disparity between the four billion Gentiles in the world today and only fifteen or sixteen million Jews, the number of Jews will probably be comparable to the total number of Gentiles who enter the millennium.

The other group of people who will occupy the millennium will do so in their resurrected bodies. They will not procreate, but they will rule with Christ during that period. Only those who exist in their natural bodies will continue to have the power to procreate.

A Time of Righteousness

One fact stands out in bold relief regarding the millennial kingdom: it will be a time of righteousness and justice. One of the clearest descriptions of the righteous, characteristic of the Kingdom Age, appears in Isaiah 11:1-5:

And there shall come forth a rod out of the stem of Jesse, and a Branch shall grow out of his roots: And the spirit of the Lord shall rest upon him, the spirit of wisdom and understanding, the spirit of counsel and might, the spirit of knowledge and of the fear of the Lord; And shall make him of quick understanding in the fear of the Lord: and he shall not judge after the sight of his eyes, neither reprove after the hearing of his ears: But with righteousness shall he judge the poor, and reprove with equity for the meek of the earth: and he shall smite the earth with the rod of his mouth, and with the breath of his lips shall he slay the wicked. And righteousness shall be the girdle of his loins, and faithfulness the girdle of his reins.

The millennial kingdom will be an age of righteousness for two reasons. One is that Christ, the holy and righteous God-judge, will be the sovereign. He will tolerate nothing less than righteousness. The other (Revelation 20:1-3) is that Satan will be bound in the bottomless pit, "that he should deceive the nations no more till the thousand years were finished." Satan has always been the master deceiver, ever since his attack on Eve in Genesis 3. He has tried to delude us into thinking that the laws of God are harmful. Modern trends, inspired by Satan through humanist philosophers of evil, advocate sexual promiscuity, unlimited alcohol consumption, drug addiction, abortion, mercy killing, pornography, and everything else that is contrary to the will of God.

Can you imagine living in a kingdom where it is illegal to sell alcoholic beverages, harmful drugs, or pornographic literature? Can you envision an earthly domain without prostitution, divorce, or any of the other society-destroying evils of our times? Such will be the case during the kingdom era of Christ.

Population Explosion

No one knows how large the population will be at the beginning of the millennium. Because of God's judgments on the earth during the tribulation, the world's population may be reduced substantially, then increase rapidly. Isaiah 65:19-22 indicates that it will be a time of permanence: one who builds a house will not have to worry about the government stealing it from him through taxation or even confiscation, nor will he have to fear his fellowman. One who sows a field will be assured of reaping his own harvest.

It will also be a time of longevity, for according to verse 20, "There shall be no more thence an infant of days, nor an old man that hath not filled his days: for the child shall die an hundred years old; but the sinner being an hundred years old shall be accursed." From this we deduce that the age span of man will revert back to what it was in the days of Adam, who lived 930 years; or Methuselah, 969; or Noah, 950. A person one hundred years of age will be considered only a child. Verse 20 also prophesies that a child and a sinner dying at one hundred years of age are considered synonymous. Bible scholars take this to mean that if a person reaches his one hundredth birthday and does not receive Christ, he dies. Therefore the people who live to their two hundredth, or six hundredth, or eight hundredth year, propagating and raising generations of children, will all be Christians.

It is reasonable to assume, then, that the vast majority of people living during this era will be born-again Christians. If we believers today can raise our children successfully in the faith with all of the forces of evil aimed at the family, Christians during that age will certainly be able to do so. Not only will the government be one of righteousness and cooperation with the family, but the culture will advocate morality and decency, and Satan will not be on hand to deceive or tempt mankind. Since only Christians will be able to propagate after their one hundredth birthday, we will see a reverse of the statistics that exist worldwide today of a few million Christians and several billion non-Christians.

At this time the Jews will accept Christ as their Messiah, and a new heart will be given to them. The Gentiles who befriended them at the risk of their own lives during the tribulation will be much like Cornelius in Acts 10. They will have responded to the gospel the first time they heard it in truth. These are evidently God-fearing, open-hearted people who have just never heard the gospel at the time of the judgment of the nations.

The Universal Knowledge of God

Behold, the days come, saith the Lord, that I will make a new covenant with the house of Israel and with the house of Judah: Not according to the covenant that I made with their fathers in the day that I took them by the hand to bring them out of the land of Egypt; which my covenant they brake, although I was an husband unto them, saith the Lord: But this shall be the covenant that I will make with the house of Israel; after those days, saith the Lord, I will put my law in their inward parts, and write it in their hearts; and will be their God, and they shall be my people. And they shall teach no more every man his neighbour, and every man his brother, saying, Know the Lord: for they shall all know me, from the least of them unto the greatest of them, saith the Lord: for I will forgive their iniquity, and I will remember their sin no more (Jeremiah 31:31-34).

One of the characteristics of our time is that so few people know about the God of the Bible. That will not be the case during the millennium, however, as the prophet Jeremiah tells us, "For they shall all know me, from the least of them unto the greatest of them, saith the Lord: for I will forgive their iniquity, and I will remember their sin no more." During the millennium it will not be necessary for Christians to go witnessing door to door, because their neighbors will know the gospel as well as they do. You can easily see how this universal knowledge of the gospel will also help to produce a worldwide population of Christians.

An Era of Peace

Here is one of the best known verses in relationship to the millennium. "And he shall judge among the nations, and shall rebuke many people: and they shall beat their swords into plowshares, and their spears into pruninghooks: nation shall not lift up sword against nation, neither shall they learn war any more" (Isaiah 2:4). Man's insatiable and nearly universal craving for world peace will be fulfilled during the millennium. No one will be able to stand in opposition to the King of kings and Lord of lords. Consequently, man will not make war anymore. This in itself will contribute to the population explosion, because the flower of each nation's youth will not be consumed in senseless killing.

A Period of Abundance

Most population control enthusiasts would shudder in horror at the enormity of the population explosion that will exist during the millennium. In fact, they wouldn't know how to cope with the idea that the millennium may well duplicate the aggregate population of the entire world. Naturally, the first thought that comes to mind is, "Where will these people get enough food in order to live?" The answer to that question is very simple: the curse will be lifted.

The wolf also shall dwell with the lamb, and the leopard shall lie down with the kid; and the calf and the young lion and the fatling together; and a little child shall lead them. And the cow and the bear shall feed; their young ones shall lie down together: and the lion shall eat straw like the ox. And the sucking child shall play on the hole of the asp, and the weaned child shall put his hand on the cockatrice den. They shall not hurt nor destroy in all my holy mountain: for the earth shall be full of the knowledge of the Lord, as the waters cover the sea (Isaiah 11:6-9).

CHAPTER SIX

THE SECOND
RESURRECTION

Daniel Webster, the great statesman, attended a luncheon accompanied by a group of younger men. During the meal the conversation dwindled to small talk, so Mr. Webster began to write at the side of his plate while others conversed. In an effort to include their senior guest, the chairman of the group interrupted the discussion by inquiring, "Mr. Webster, what is the greatest thought that ever passed through your mind?" Without a moment's hesitation the wise old man replied, "My accountability to God!"

Actually, when all of education, theory, science, and philosophy are considered, what is more important than man's accountability to God? In Romans 14:12 we find, "So then each of us shall give account of himself to God." The Bible predicts that a day is coming when every man will stand before God to give an account of himself. As we have seen, the believer will stand at what the Bible calls the Judgment Seat of Christ (2 Corinthians 5:10). The unbeliever, however, will appear before the Great White Throne Judgment (Revelation 20:11-15).

Written intuitively on the table of every man's heart is the knowledge that one day he will be ushered into God's presence in order to give an account of himself. One of the reasons many agnostics, humanists, and unbelievers refuse to acknowledge the existence of God is that they are subconsciously afraid of one day facing him at the judgment. Unfortunately for them, disbelief has nothing to do with it, for the Bible is abundantly clear that after death comes judgment. "And as it is appointed for men to die once, but after this the judgment" (Hebrews 9:27).

The fact of judgment in the afterlife is not a teaching unique to Christianity. It was taught clearly in the Old Testament, but it is interesting that the most frequent mention of this event came from the lips of Jesus Christ, who one day will be the judge before whom men and women will stand.

Jesus on Judgment

Jesus used a parable to describe this ultimate judgment of those who choose not to accept his gift of salvation. He told of a man who sowed good seed in his field. But while he was sleeping, his enemy sneaked over and sowed weeds among the wheat. When the wheat took root and grew, the weeds flourished right along with it. When this was discovered, the servants asked the man if they should pull up the weeds. "No," he answered, "let them all grow together until the harvest. At that time we will have the reapers collect the weeds and burn them. Then we will gather the wheat and bring it into my barn."

Matthew 13:37-43 contains Jesus' explanation of this parable. The field is the world, the good seed are the children of the kingdom, and the weeds (or "tares") are the children of the wicked one, or the ungodly. Notice in verse 39 that the devil is the one who sowed the tares, the harvest is the end of the world, and the reapers are God's angels. In verse 40 Jesus predicted, "Therefore as the tares are gathered and burned in the fire, so it will be at the end of this age. The Son of Man will send out His angels, and they will gather out of His kingdom all things that offend, and those who practice lawlessness, and will cast them into the furnace of fire. There will be wailing and gnashing of teeth." This is one of the most basic parables in the Bible, and it presents a graphic picture of the unbeliever who, though he may be religious, is really a "tare" or a seed of the devil who will be judged in the harvest at the end of the world.

The Time of This Judgment

The Great White Throne Judgment occurs at the end of the millennial kingdom, after Satan has led his insurrection and failed. Satan, the beast, and the false prophet have already been thrown into the Lake of Fire. As you look at the chart on page 31, you find this judgment located at the extreme end of the time line just before the beginning of the ages to come. These ages are called the new heaven and the new earth and are predicted in Revelation 21, 22. The last event, then, just before the Heaven Jesus promised to prepare, is the Great White Throne Judgment, described as follows:

And I saw a great white throne and Him who sat on it, from whose face the earth and the heaven fled away. And there was found no place for them. And I saw the dead, small and great, standing before God, and books were opened. And another book was opened, which is the Book of Life. And the dead were judged according to their works by the things which were written in the books. And the sea gave up the dead who were in it, and Death and Hades delivered up the dead who were in them. And they were judged, each one according to his works. And Death and Hades were cast into the lake of fire. This is the second death. And anyone not found written in the Book of Life was cast into the lake of fire (Rev. 20:11-15).

On a flight from Salt Lake City to San Francisco I was seated next to a salesman who claimed he had never read a Bible. The closest he had been to church in his life was to drop his daughter off at the Congregational church every other week for Sunday school on his way to the golf course. I asked him if he would submit to an experiment, to which he agreed. Many people say the Bible is a difficult book to understand, particularly Revelation. Turning to the above passage, I handed him my Bible with only a brief instruction: "This is a prophecy about a future event." I waited as he read.

His joyful mood changed abruptly, and soon he exclaimed, "If that's true, I'd better get right with God."

That salesman put into words the main reason God has given us so much information about the afterlife judgment that awaits all those who reject or neglect God. As an aid to the following comments on this awesome passage in Revelation, we shall examine the details on the next few pages very carefully. The chart on the following page is an artist's concept of that event. Please compare it with the description as we proceed.

We have already seen in Acts 17:30, 31 that God will judge the world by "that man whom he hath ordained." We may well ask, whom has he ordained? Is it God the Father, as some people think? The answer appears in the latter part of the verse: Whom he has "raised from the dead." The Lord Jesus Christ is the only person in world history who can match this description. He is the only one who could judge the world "in righteousness," for only he is "without sin" (1 Peter 2:22).

John 5:22 confirms Christ's identity as the judge, since Jesus said, "For the Father judges no one, but has committed all judgment to the Son." Therefore we come to the irrefutable conclusion that the judge who sits on the Great White Throne is none other than the Lord Jesus Christ himself. The very person who was rejected and scorned will ultimately sit in judgment on them. That is a very sobering thought!

One imposing feature of Christ being the judge is that even on this earth in his human body he had the incredible ability to look at a person and know him intimately. You can be sure no individual will be able to hide himself from the Savior's penetrating eye on judgment day. For as the Bible says, "There is no creature hidden from His sight, but all things are naked and open to the eyes of Him to whom we must give account" (Hebrews 4:13). We also read, "Therefore do not fear them. For there is nothing covered that will not be revealed, and hidden that will not be known" (Matthew 10:26).

GREAT
WHITE THRONE
JUDGMENT
REVELATION 20:10-15

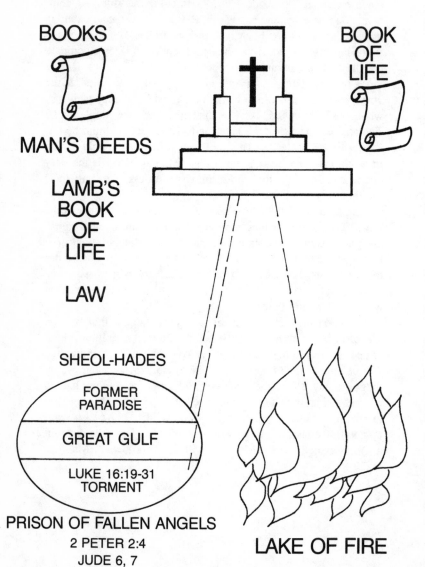

BOOKS

BOOK OF LIFE

MAN'S DEEDS

LAMB'S
BOOK
OF
LIFE

LAW

SHEOL-HADES

FORMER
PARADISE

GREAT GULF

LUKE 16:19-31
TORMENT

PRISON OF FALLEN ANGELS
2 PETER 2:4
JUDE 6, 7

LAKE OF FIRE

Who Appears at This Judgment?

Now that we have verified the identity of the judge, we may inquire
as to the identity of those to be judged. John reports in Revelation
20:12, "And I saw the dead, small and great, standing before
God." It is significant to note that all those who stand at the Great
White Throne Judgment are the "dead"—dead in trespasses and
sins because of their rejection of Jesus Christ, resurrected in order
to appear at this judgment. "The rest of the dead [that is, those who
were not raised before the beginning of the thousand years] did not
live again until the thousand years were finished" (Revelation
20:5). Note that the dead are referred to as "small and great." God,
who is no respecter of persons, judges fairly without regard to
status—intellectually, physically, financially, or positionally.

What many people do not understand is that all unbelievers are
"dead" spiritually even while they are alive. Jesus said to the
Jews, "I have come that they may have life, and that they may have
it more abundantly" (John 10:10). That is an incredible statement.
Those Jews, like all unbelievers, thought they had life but were
like the woman mentioned earlier by Paul "who was dead while
she lives." That is, she was alive physically but dead spiritually.

Unbelievers go to torment or the place called "death" when
they die because they have no spiritual life in them. As the chart
on page 31 shows, they remain there until judgment day, when
they are brought before Christ, whom they have rejected, as he sits
on the Great White Throne.

Many through the years have shared a common misconception
of judgment day by stating their philosophy as follows: "When
I stand before God, he will put the bad things I've done on one side
of the scale and balance it with my good deeds. If my good works
outweigh my bad, I've made it; if not, I haven't." Little do such
individuals realize that God regards their good works, the very
best deeds they have performed, as "filthy rags."

Other living "dead" people will appear at that judgment thinking that they will be saved somehow because they are good, kind,

lovable people who live by the Golden Rule, have spent a lifetime as church members, or "do the best I can." If they concede the existence of a hell at all, it is strictly for all kinds of vile people —whoremongers, adulterers, criminals, murderers. They do not seem to remember or admit to the biblical teaching that hell was intended to house unbelievers. People regularly ask, "What about the heathen? Will a righteous God condemn the heathen who have never heard about hell?" Remember that many heathen are idolaters, and Revelation 21:8 tells us that " . . .idolaters and all liars shall have their part in the lake which burns with fire and brimstone, which is the second death." They are not only idolaters, but unbelievers, so they are doubly condemned.

Still another group of the "dead small and great" will be the religious who have never been saved. Matthew 7:21-23 says, "Not everyone who says to Me, 'Lord, Lord,' will enter the kingdom of heaven, but he who does the will of My Father who is in heaven. Many will say to Me in that day, 'Lord, Lord, have we not prophesied in Your name, cast out demons in Your name, and done many wonderful works in Your name?' And then I will declare to them, 'I never knew you; depart from Me, you who practice lawlessness!' " This is one of the most staggering passages to be found in the Word of God. The Lord Jesus is speaking here about religious people who say unto him, "Lord, Lord." They claim that they have prophesied and cast out devils in his name, performing many wonderful works. What is their trouble? The answer is clear in verse 23. Jesus said, "I never knew you." I cannot think of more awesome words being pronounced on a human being at the Great White Throne Judgment. Oh, the misery and heartache and eternal tragedy that will attend upon the Lord Jesus Christ's statement: "I never knew you."

We might well ask, why is it that he never knew them? Because they had never been born again. Jesus told Nicodemus in John 3:3, "Unless one is born again, he cannot see the kingdom of God." This country of ours, in fact the whole world, is filled with "religious" people who profess to be Christians but have never been "born again." They have never acknowledged their personal sins and called upon the name of the Lord for salvation. On a religious impulse they may have joined the church and even buried themselves in Christian works, but being baptized, being confirmed, giving a tithe, or serving as a church officer cannot be equated with becoming a Christian. That is simply man's religiosity. Just as Adam and Eve were naked in the eyes of God in spite of covering themselves with fig leaves, and therefore God had to provide his own covering which involved a blood sacrifice, so men cannot gild their sins with moral works and church membership. To all of these Jesus will say at that hour, "Depart from me, I never knew you." If any teaching in the Word of God should make a man examine his own personal sin, it is this. If he has any doubt that he has ever accepted Christ, such an individual needs to call upon the name of the Lord and be saved.

Verse 13 of Revelation 20 adds another bit of description about these "dead" people when it tells us that "the sea gave up the dead who were in it, and Death and Hades delivered up the dead who were in them." The sea relinquishes all those who were drowned at sea, never having accepted Jesus Christ. These two verses teach that there is a physical resurrection with eternal spiritual life (study Ephesians 3). Whether their ashes are in the grave, in a mausoleum, on the earth, or in the sea, God will resurrect his creatures to their original bodies, souls, and spirits. Their remains will be resurrected and united with the soul and spirit as they come up out of the Place of Torment, and in this resurrected form they will stand "before the throne."

Many unbelievers choose not to believe what God has said regarding the basis for judgment—the acceptance or rejection of his Son. They consider themselves "as good as the next person" and insist that hell—if it exists at all—must have been created for thieves and murderers. That may be true, but hell will likewise be full of many "not too bad" people who scorned the love of God as demonstrated through the sacrificial death of his beloved Son. Matthew 7:21-23 tells the sad story of some very religious people who showed great confidence in their works but were told by Jesus, "I never knew you." What misery, what heartache, what tragedy it will be for some to hear in that hour of final, irrevocable judgment, "Depart from me, I never knew you."

The Various Books of Judgment

"And books were opened... And the dead were judged according to their works, by the things which were written in the books" (Revelation 20:12). Evidently God owns a complete set of books that record every transaction of man's life, waiting to be recalled on judgment day. It may be that each of us has a recording angel who in this life is transcribing everything we do. In connection with this thought, it is well to consider Ecclesiastes 12:14, "For God shall bring every work into judgment, with every secret thing, whether it be good, or whether it be evil." In this final hour the books of man's works (his deeds) will be open. If a mortal being is able by the means of photography to capture the action of a man's life and by the means of recordings replay man's voice, certainly Almighty God can do the same. I have often been amazed at the retrieval system of modern computers. Certainly if man can locate and reestablish millions of bits of information, the supreme God can do no less.

Not only the actions but the words of man will be recalled at this judgment; Ecclesiastes 12:14 specifies that "every secret thing" will be included. This would indicate that God has a special X-ray-like camera which takes photographs of the thoughts and intents of the heart, prefatory to revealing those "secret things" in that day. Dr. D. L. Moody, the famous evangelist, used to say that if a man ever invented a camera that could take a picture of the human heart, he would starve to death, since people would refuse to reveal the inner recesses of their being. In that awesome day all the secret thoughts and intents of the heart will be revealed by the projection of God's special playback, taken from each man's personal book of deeds.

No Secrets from God

"Every secret thing" shall be brought into judgment. Many people have the mistaken idea that because they have escaped the penalty of sin in this world, it has gone unnoticed. This is far from the truth. The Scripture tells us, "The eyes of God run to and fro in the earth." No act of wickedness eludes the all-seeing eye of God. Many a man has lived his life of shame in secret. On the surface he was highly respected and regarded, loved by his family and friends, but in reality he had sustained a secret sin which if discovered would have ostracized him from the family. In that day that secret sin will be revealed. Many a murderer has gone free because it was impossible to identify him. Our courts of law frequently release criminals on mere technicalities.

Recently I read that in the city of London a self-confessed murderer was freed to walk the streets. He had been tried for his murder and found innocent, but after the trial admitted his guilt. Because English law states that a man cannot be tried for a crime twice, he was not threatened by double jeopardy. But that is only true in this life. Many an unfaithful woman goes about in society representing herself as a model of virtue and purity, even though she has committed the scarlet sin of adultery or fornication. Although she is able to hide her sins from men, she has not concealed her guilt from God, and it will be revealed in that day. Nothing you have ever done has escaped the all-seeing eye of God, as recorded in the Books of Man's Works. I remind you that at the Great White Throne Judgment every man shall be judged "according to his works."

Seated in a San Diego courtroom, I saw a graphic foreglimpse of Judgment Day. I had been summoned to appear as a witness for a woman being divorced by her serviceman husband. He refused to give her and their children a reasonable financial settlement and was very cocky and self-assured during his testimony. To prove his infidelity, his wife produced a roll of 8mm movie film she had found in his belongings, taken of his Chinese mistress with whom he had lived in Taiwan during a tour of duty. The change in his facial expression was incredible as he watched his private sin flashed on the screen. Needless to say, he huddled with his attorney, they requested a conference in the judge's chambers, and immediately the case was settled out of court. As I drove home that day, I realized a little of the awesomeness of judgment, when "every secret thing" that is contrary to God will be revealed.

"But I say to you, that for every idle word men may speak, they will give account of it in the day of judgment" (Matt. 12:36). This statement fell from the lips of the Lord Jesus Christ and presents the truth that "every idle word" is subject to the Day of Judgment. All my life I have heard profane men, particularly those who blasphemed the name of Jesus Christ, explain, "I don't really mean what I say," or, "It's just an idle habit." What they do not realize is that "for every idle word men may speak, they will give account of it in the day of judgment." The Bible says, "The Lord will not hold him guiltless that taketh his name in vain." All the smutty stories, all the filthy speech, all the idle criticism shall be openly displayed in that day, for it is recorded in the "Books of Man's Works."

"Do not be deceived, God is not mocked; for whatever a man sows that he will also reap. For he who sows to his flesh will of the flesh reap corruption, but he who sows to the Spirit will of the Spirit reap everlasting life." This passage suggests the minuteness of that recording, for how else could man "reap what he has sown"? This verse also demonstrates the need for a day of judgment, for its warranty is not always fulfilled in this life. People sow selfishness, wickedness, and dishonesty to the profit of the flesh in this life, and many of them die and seemingly never are judged. Why? Because we are not always judged in this life. Judgment is reserved for the Great White Throne, which determines a man's degree of punishment in hell.

Just as man intuitively knows that he will stand before God someday, he also realizes that he will be judged in relation to the Law of God. Galatians 3:10 confirms that consciousness when it says, "For as many as are of the works of the law are under the curse; for it is written, 'Cursed is everyone who does not continue

in all things which are written in the book of the law, to do them.' "
This is the first verse we have considered that predicates degrees of
punishment, for it does not tell us that all men are under the works
of the law and thus "under the curse," but says "for as many as are
of the works of the law"—that is, some people are not under the
works of the law, for they have never heard of the law of God. This,
of course, is in harmony with Romans 2:12: "For as many as have
sinned without law will also perish without law, and as many as
have sinned in the law will be judged by the law." These verses
make it clear that those who have never heard the law will be judged
on the basis that they have never heard it, whereas those who have
heard the law will be judged accordingly.

Now notice in Galatians 3:10 the tremendous responsibility
which rests upon the one who has heard the law. The law of God
will confront every man who stands before the Lord Jesus at the
Great White Throne. In that hour, if he has heard the law, he will
be held accountable for every single part of it and for individual
transgressions of it; he is told that a curse is pronounced upon
everyone that "does not continue in all things which are written
in the book of the law, to do them." The appearance here of the law
of God will certainly suffice to condemn a man, even to himself.
He may tell his friends that he keeps the law of God and think that
he has deceived them (though usually he does not), but he will
certainly not have the affrontery to stand before the Lord Jesus
Christ himself and claim that he has upheld the law of God.

Are There Degrees of Punishment?

The above-mentioned verse of Scripture also implies that there are
degrees of punishment in hell. Isaiah 45:21 tells us that God is a just
God, and Hebrews 2:2 advises us that "every transgression and
disobedience received a just reward." Because of the justice of
God, we can be certain that he will not treat the heathen, those who
have never heard the gospel of Jesus Christ, with the same
judgment as the man who has listened to the message hundreds of
times and rejected it. Neither will he recompense the fine moral

citizen (doctor, teacher, good neighbor) who has lived a comparatively good life (though short of the standard of God) the same as he would Adolph Hitler, under whose regime six million of God's chosen people were slain.

Matthew 11:21-24 shows us that those with extensive opportunity to receive the truth, but who reject it, are subject to greater condemnation than those who have never heard. The cities mentioned—cities in which Christ did many of his mighty works—were compared to the wicked cities of Sodom and Gomorrah, Tyre and Sidon. They will be much more severely judged because of their refusal to believe the truth. To say "it will be more tolerable for Tyre and Sidon in the day of judgment" than for Chorazin, where he had taught and performed many miracles, establishes the fact that those who have heard the gospel and rejected it will fall into greater judgment than the homosexual sinners in Sodom.

In Luke 12:42-48, God's justice and mercy are evident in the parable of the steward and his servants. Verse 47 establishes the fact that the servant who "knew his master's will and did not prepare himself, nor do according to his will, shall be beaten with many stripes." In verse 48, the opposite is true. He who did not know his lord's will and committed things worthy of stripes shall be "beaten with few." By analogy, all those who ignore the gospel and refuse to turn to Christ for salvation and forgiveness of sins will be "beaten with many stripes." They will be the ones who suffer most grievously in hell, for Jesus said, "For everyone to whom much is given, from him much will be required." Without any question, there will be degrees of punishment in hell—as certain as the fact that God is a just God (Genesis 18:25).

It is imperative that every unbeliever recognize the truth that the Lord Jesus Christ will hold him accountable in proportion to the degree of opportunity he has had. The gospel of Jesus Christ is preached in every city and is available by radio, television or printed page to almost everyone in the western world. The recording angel knows and records all the times that the gospel has been heard by an individual.

To be sure, no part of hell will be a desirable place, for it is all a place of torment, but the position of the heathen who has never heard the gospel will be like heaven compared with your place if you reject his "so great salvation."

Does all of this paint a rather hopeless picture for you? Does the prospect of judgment frighten you? Well, let me pause here to point out a marvelous truth, the greatest truth that can ever be proclaimed upon the earth. In view of the fact that all men will one day have to stand before God to give an account of everything they have ever done, the greatest news in the world is that Jesus Christ has died on Calvary's cross so that the books of our works can be destroyed! The Bible promises, "If we confess our sins, He is faithful and just to forgive us our sins and to cleanse us from all unrighteousness" (1 John 1:9). Think of it—through the blood of Christ we can be cleansed from all sin. The pages of the books of our works can be completely erased. When I contemplate the fearsome prospect of the Great White Throne Judgment, I can never thank God enough for the wonderful joy I can have in my heart because the awful record of my sins has been totally destroyed through Christ.

THE BOOKS OF LIFE

BOOK OF LIFE

LAMB'S BOOK OF LIFE

Now it is time to examine the two most important books that await every man's encounter with God. Although they are similar, they also bear significant differences.

While going to conduct a funeral service at the Cypress View Mausoleum in San Diego, I walked down the corridor to the chapel with the funeral director and read the names of the deceased engraved on marble slabs bolted to the wall. We passed a small library section where I could see several books standing on end. Intrigued by the books, I stepped in to get a closer look. There I saw books entitled "The

Book of Life," under which were inscribed in gold letters the names of the deceased. Turning to the funeral director, I asked him if these metallic, book-shaped containers held the ashes of the deceased. He assured me that they did. Then I asked, "Do you tell folks that if they have their ashes placed on one of your containers, their names are written in the Book of Life that will be opened at the Great White Throne Judgment?" The poor man looked flustered and confessed that he didn't know.

These sincere souls probably paid a premium price to have their ashes placed in such a container. It is unfortunate that they failed to check with the Bible first, because it is crystal clear on this matter. In the day of judgment, their ashes will be stirred by God, forming a resurrected body which will be united with their souls, and they will stand before the Great White Throne Judgment— only to find that their names do *not* appear in the Book of Life. Having one's ashes placed in a container does not insure that one's name is written in the Book of Life. What we do with this old body after the spirit and soul have left is of no vital concern. Of primary importance is what we have done with Jesus Christ *before* death, since that alone determines whether or not our names will appear in the Book of Life.

The New Testament refers to the Book of Life eight different times, and although the Old Testament does not call it by that name, it does allude three times to a book in which names are written. The psalmist speaks of the righteous as having their names in "the book of the living" (Psalm 69:28), so we perceive that it is a book in which righteous people have their names written.

Revelation 13:8 tells us about the other Book of Life—the Book of Life of the Lamb. "The Lamb" is without doubt the Lord Jesus Christ, for only he is the "Lamb of God which taketh away the sins of the world." Because Christ came into the world to save sinners and to give them eternal life, the Lamb's Book of Life is the book of Jesus Christ in which are entered the names of those who have received his eternal life. (I am inclined to believe that this is a book in which only the believers who have lived since the cross have their names written.)

The above-mentioned verse indicates that during the tribulation period, people whose names are not written in the Lamb's book will worship the antichrist. During that period, all men will bear a mark. The worshipers of the antichrist who have rejected the Savior will carry the mark of the beast—666. Those who have turned to Christ (in this case, the 144,000) will feature a mark that is the Lamb's Father's "name written in their foreheads" (Revelation 14:1). The believers in Revelation 13:8 do not worship the beast because their names are written in the Book of the Lamb. Revelation 21:27 tells us that the only people who will enter into the Holy City are "those who are written in the Lamb's Book of Life." It is absolutely essential to one's eternal destiny whether or not his name is written in the Lamb's Book of Life.

The major difference between the two books is that the Book of Life seems to contain the names of all living people, whereas the Lamb's Book of Life includes only the names of those who call upon the Lamb for salvation. A second difference is that the Book of Life is referred to as God the Father's book in Exodus 32:33; it records all those whom God the Creator has made. It is, then, the Book of the Living, much like the county records book. On the other hand, the Lamb's Book of Life is referred to as God the Son's book (Revelation 13:8). We may conclude, then, that this book contains names of all those who have received the new life that the Son provides. The third and most important difference between these books is that one may have his name blotted out of the Book of Life, but not the Lamb's Book of Life. According to Exodus 32:33, "The Lord said unto Moses, Whosoever hath sinned against me, him will I blot out of my book." It is possible, therefore, to have one's name erased from the Book of Life because of sin.

The Lamb's Book of Life is different, however. Revelation 3:5 promises, "He who overcomes shall be clothed in white garments, and I will not blot out his name from the Book of Life . . ." An overcomer here is one who is clothed in the white garments of Christ; the Creator has imputed to him divine righteousness, and his name cannot be blotted out of the Lamb's Book of Life.

There is yet another way in which we can have our names removed from the Book of Life. Revelation 22:19 explains, 'And if anyone takes away from the words of the book of this prophecy, God will take away his part from the Book of Life, from the holy city, and from the things which are written in this book." Some try to convince us that whoever detracts from the book of Revelation and its prophecy will lose his part out of the Book of Life and will also forfeit his rewards. This simply cannot be, for the only "part" we have in the Book of Life is our name. Scripture does not indicate that anything but our name is written there, because the deeds of a man are only recorded in the books of our works.

Thus we may determine three reasons for having one's name blotted out of the Book of Life: 1) for sinning against God, 2) for not being clothed in the righteousness of Christ through the new birth, and 3) for taking "away from the words of the book of this prophecy."

Primarily because a man's name can be blotted out of the Book of Life, I am convinced that the Book of Life and the Lamb's Book of Life are not the same book. As we have seen, the Lamb's Book contains the names of all those who have been born again through the shed blood of the Lamb, and we know from many passages of Scripture that it is impossible for anyone who has once been born again to lose his salvation. Therefore we can be sure that these are two distinctly separate books. The Book of Life is that book in which the names of all people ever born into the world are written. If, at the time of their death, they have not called upon the Lord Jesus Christ for salvation, their names are blotted out of the Book of Life. If they *have* accepted Christ and his forgiveness of sins, their names are indelibly recorded in the Lamb's Book of Life, and entrance into the Holy City is guaranteed (Revelation 21:27).

We have spent quite some time discussing the Book of Life, but in order to grasp its importance, we need only look at Revelation 20:15: "And anyone not found written in the Book of Life was cast into the lake of fire." In a sense, this is God's double-check at the Great White Throne Judgment. As a man comes forward, he is judged by the Book of the Law, by the Books of his works, and by the Lamb's Book of Life. Then, just before he receives his sentence, he is given a double-check. The recording angel will refer to the book, and anyone not found written in the Book of Life will be thrown into the lake of fire. The Bible repeatedly contrasts two kinds of people, using such words as "believing" and "unbelieving," "saved" and "unsaved," "condemned" and "not condemned," "righteous" and "unrighteous," "just" and "unjust," etc. The principle is maintained in names being written or not written in the Book of Life. In that hour, there will be no hesitation or question, for a man's name is either written or not written—it must be one way or the other.

When I was stationed at Las Vegas Army Air Base, awaiting gunnery school training, I was very restless to go home. It was common procedure that immediately after the ten-week gunnery school, a thirty-day furlough was granted. Every Friday we would run to the bulletin board to see if the new roster of trainees contained our names. Some of the boys returned from the bulletin board joyfully, some sorrowfully, all based on whether or not their name was written on the roster. It was not debatable. Either the name appeared or it did not. The same is true in the judgment day, except that far more than a thirty-day furlough is involved.

You need not try to enter your name in the Book of Life, for it is already there because of God's will that none "should perish but that all should come to repentance." To keep it there, you must have your name written in the Lamb's Book of Life as a result of coming to the Lamb.

Jesus Christ said, "I am the bread of life. He who comes to Me shall never hunger, and he who believes on Me shall never thirst" (John 6:35). Repeatedly, the Lord Jesus invites men to come to him, for he alone is "the way, the truth, and the life." John 5:24 tells us, "Most assuredly, I say to you, he who hears My word and believes in Him who sent Me has everlasting life, and shall not come into judgment, but has passed from death into life." The steps of salvation are very clear: 1) "he who hears My word" and 2) "believes in Him who sent Me." That means trusting on him. Trust that Jesus Christ is the way of salvation, the one who has come to "seek and to save that which was lost"—including you —and to give you everlasting life. Those whose names are written in the Lamb's Book of Life have received this everlasting life. Have you? Your answer to that question determines your eternal destiny.

Many of the saints who have accepted him suffer from "eternal insecurity," often not being able to enjoy their salvation for fear of losing it. Recently here at Christian Heritage College, in San Diego, a guest speaker said, "Aren't you glad the song doesn't go, 'There's a new name written down *in pencil*'?" Although he was obviously jesting, the question contains a truth. Our Lord has saved us for all eternity. The apostle Paul wrote, "He who has begun a good work in you will complete it until the day of Christ Jesus."

While pastoring in Minnesota, I had the joy of leading a businessman named Bob to Christ one Monday evening. I had spoken on the Revelation passage in church the day before, which evidently influenced his decision and his prayer. After admitting his sin to God and inviting Christ into his life, he then added, almost like a postscript, "And Lord, please write my name in the Lamb's Book of Life." Although I'm confident that God knew what he meant, my friend Bob didn't have to say that, for one's name is automatically registered whenever a person calls on the name of the Lord to be saved.

One Last Formality

One awesome event recorded in Philippians is rarely mentioned in this connection, but it should be. The apostle Paul wrote,

Therefore God also has highly exalted Him and given Him the name which is above every name, that at the name of Jesus every knee should bow, of those in heaven, and of those on earth, and of those under the earth, and that every tongue should confess that Jesus Christ is Lord, to the glory of God the Father (Philippians 2:9-11).

After giving a wonderful description of how Christ was willing to humble himself and "become obedient to the point of death, even the death of the cross," Paul warns that there is a day coming when every knee shall bow and every tongue confess that Jesus Christ is Lord. All the skeptics, all the infidels, all the procrastinators, and all the rejectors of Christ will acknowledge that Jesus Christ is Lord! The believers in heaven, those dead who had rejected him, and those living on the earth at his coming—all will bow to him and acknowledge that he is Christ the Lord.

You too, will acknowledge him. You may have rejected him, and you may go out into eternity rejecting him, but there is a day coming when you *will* acknowledge him. However, if you wait until then, it will be too late. "Now is the accepted time, today is the day of salvation."

CHAPTER SEVEN

IS THE AFTERLIFE ALWAYS ETERNAL?

So far we have learned that there is a place in the heart of the earth called Sheol-Hades, where all the dead went before the time of Christ. That place was divided by the "Great Gulf Fixed" into two main compartments: The Place of Comfort (or Paradise) and the Place of Torment. The wicked and the unbelieving went to the Place of Torment, the believers to the Place of Comfort. After the Lord Jesus died on the cross, he descended into the heart of the earth; as implied in Ephesians 4:8-10, he set the Old Testament believers free and took them to Paradise to be with himself. Now when a saint dies, "to be absent from the body is to be present with the Lord." Therefore at the present time there are two places for the dead. The unbelievers still go to the Place of Torment in Sheol-Hades, but the believers are translated to the Place of Paradise, which is now "present with the Lord." The compartment in Sheol-Hades marked "comfort" is now empty.

We have seen, in addition, that many activities are reserved for the believer. He will face the Judgment Seat of Christ, he will rule with him during the millennium, and finally he will occupy the Holy City that will come down out of heaven. Let us not forget, however, that the fate of unbelievers is appalling. Revelation

20:11-15 points out that immediately after the resurrection, they will be brought up out of Sheol-Hades to stand before the Lord Jesus Christ and be judged "according to their works." "And anyone not found written in the Book of Life was cast into the lake of fire." The Lake of Fire, then, becomes the final dwelling place of the unbelieving dead.

Unpleasant Subject

Teaching which focuses on the "Lake of Fire" or "hell" (as it is called in the Bible) is most unpopular. For some reason the modern pulpit is strangely silent on this subject. Naturally, it is much more pleasant to preach on heaven than on hell because people enjoy hearing about all the blessings that a future with God will insure. However, the same Bible that declares the glories of heaven also forecasts the torments of hell. As wonderful as heaven is, just so terrifying is the place called hell. If the minister of Jesus Christ does not warn men about this awful place, who will? In fact, refusal to proclaim this warning carries with it a solemn penalty. Ezekiel 3:18 gives clear direction on this matter: "When I say unto the wicked, Thou shalt surely die; and thou givest him not warning, or speakest to warn the wicked from his wicked way, to save his life; the same wicked man shall die in his iniquity; but his blood will I require at thine hand."

If I were your doctor and reported that you were suffering from an incurable disease and had only four months to live, you would thank me for telling you the truth so that you could set your house in order and prepare for eternity. If I were your lawyer and informed you that your probate case was hopeless, you would value my counsel and save yourself hundreds of dollars by not taking this hopeless case into court. Why is it, then, that when a preacher of the gospel warns men of the inevitable fact of hell, he is accused of being "old-fashioned," "narrow," and "bigoted"? I'll tell you why . . .because the adversary, the devil, is anxious to deceive lost men lest they believe the truth and be saved.

The Devil's Lies

From his first appearance in the Garden of Eden to this present day, day, the devil has been busy leading people to distrust the Word of God. Whatever God says, Satan challenges. In the early chapters of Genesis Satan caused Adam and Eve to disbelieve the statement of God that if they ate of the fruit of the tree of the knowledge of good and evil, they would "surely die." Satan replied, "Thou shalt *not* surely die." This statement consequently led them progressively in the downward path until they sinned.

So it is today. The devil goes about claiming, "There is no hell," or insists that hell is just the grave or a figurative place where no literal suffering takes place. Sometimes he contends that those in hell will be given another chance to be saved after death. Perhaps he will bring up the age-old argument that, "God is too good and too loving to send his people to hell."

Although the Bible clearly teaches that all men in the Lake of Fire will be tormented day and night forever and ever, a myriad of voices today insist that hell is not eternal. The main thesis of these annihilationists is that eternal life is for those who have believed, but eternal death is just the "grave" or a place where one will be burned up. I wish I could verify from Scripture that hell does not produce eternal suffering or that people receive a second chance after death, but I could not be true to the Word of God and make such a statement. Not the slightest hint of either concept appears in the Bible. Scripture clearly and undeniably states that the Lake of Fire is eternal and that its inhabitants will be "tormented day and night forever and ever." In fact, at the time Satan is cast into the Lake of Fire, we read in Revelation 20:10 that the beast and false prophet are still there, still alive . . . *after 1,000 years!* That shows conclusively that they have the capacity to suffer indefinitely in hell and are absolutely *not* annihilated. Since they are men as we are, we can expect the same condition to be true for lost mankind.

The annihilationist also defines death as the opposite of life. He reasons that eternal life is eternal existence. Therefore, eternal death is eternal nonexistence. The Bible presents a different view of death. Ephesians 2:1 leads us to understand that before a believer is born again, he is "dead in trespasses and sins." In 1 Timothy 5:6 it tells us, "But she who lives in pleasure is dead while she lives." Thus, death is not *cessation* of existence but *wrong* existence—that is, existence contrary to the will of God. This is the plight of every unbeliever who has not received "life," the new life that comes when a person accepts Christ as Lord and Savior. The "second death," which is the Lake of Fire, comprises the eternal wrong existence of man. It is the eternal life of a man in a state that God never intended for him to experience.

The annihilationist is quick to point out that "destroy" or "perish" (they come from the same Greek word) means "consumed" or "annihilated." When the Bible tells us of a man being destroyed for rejecting Christ, they would have us believe that he is annihilated. They should reread Matthew 9:17, which tells us, "Nor do people put new wine into old wineskins; or else the wineskins break, the wine is spilled, and the wineskins will be ruined [or destroyed]. But they put new wine into new wineskins, and both are preserved." The wineskins with holes in them are not destroyed but ruined. They do not cease to be, but they do become useless in the original plan of their maker. This is exactly the position of a sinner who, upon death, is ruined in the plan of God. He will be separated from God for eternity rather than united with God forever.

Many times I have had visitors at my home trying to sell me a *Watchtower* magazine. In the course of the conversation, they always bring to my attention the statement that death is "the grave" . . .the end. This idea is clearly refuted in the Word of God. Remember how the rich man begged Abraham to permit Lazarus to go back and preach to his brothers—on the assumption that "if one goes to them from the dead, they will repent." Now follow this closely. Death could not be the grave, because no amount of repenting could ever keep a man from the grave! Even the born-again Christian who has repented of his sins and turned to Christ will be lowered into the grave (unless he happens to be alive when the Lord returns). No, death is not the grave. It is, as the rich man said, "a place of torment" to those who die outside of the Lord.

Hell Is a Fact

Hell may have lost its terror because of the modern notions of men, but it has not lost any of its reality! The place called hell is referred to fifty-three times in the New Testament alone. Actually, two words are used for hell in the King James version of the New Testament: Hades and Gehenna. In our first chapter, we established that Hades is not hell or the final place of suffering and torment; it is not the final abode of the unbelieving dead. That place is Gehenna.

Revelation 20:14 tells us that "Death and Hades were cast into the lake of fire. This is the second death." The meaning of this statement is quite clear. Death is the grave since it contains the material substance of the unbelieving dead, whereas Hades accommodates the spiritual substance of the unbelieving dead. Both will be united in the resurrection of the unbeliever, and then the place and the inhabitants will be cast into the Lake of Fire. (It is interesting to notice that the references to Hades in the New Testament are seldom as severe as the references to Gehenna, which is the Lake of Fire.)

Those who reject the doctrine of hell but are impressed by the Savior's teachings may be surprised that we receive most of our information about hell from the lips of Jesus Christ himself. It is strange that people will accept him as the divine Son of God and yet reject his teaching about hell. Remember, either he was right when he spoke about it or he was wrong. If wrong, he is not the Son of God. Someone may ask, "But why would the Son of God speak so much about that horrible place?" That is not too difficult to understand, for the Bible tells us that "all things were made by him, and without him nothing was made that was made." We will shortly examine the origin and purpose of the creation of hell, but suffice it to say here that the Lord Jesus made hell, for he created all things. Would it not follow that the one who created it, being a supernatural person and fully realizing the horrors of the place, would be more in a position to warn men to flee it than anyone else?

This thought may strike a staggering blow to some because they think of the Lord as merely a gentle spirit who preached only the Beatitudes and "God is love." We prefer to think of the Lord Jesus as displaying a compassionate heart for children, showing sympathy for the crippled and infirm, and laboring to heal those who came to him in faith. May I remind you, however, that from the lips which preached love and kindness came the teaching of Luke 12:4, 5. "And I say to you, My friends, do not be afraid of those who kill the body, and after that have no more that they can do. But I will warn you whom you should fear: Fear him who, after he has killed, has power to cast into hell; yes, I say to you, fear him!" Once again we reach the decision: are we going to believe "thus saith man" or "thus saith the Lord God"?

The Bible presents a very graphic picture of hell, which could be summed up as the complete antithesis of heaven. The eternal abode of believers is described as being so wonderful that it is beyond our ability to comprehend (1 Corinthians 2:9). Hell, on the other hand, is described as being the opposite.

Hell Described

It seems more than just coincidental that in that passage of Scripture most loved by liberals, the Sermon on the Mount, we also find Jesus' first teaching about hell (Matthew 5:29, 30). These verses not only present the horror of hell but the fact that it is a place. In verse 22 the Lord Jesus calls it a "hell of fire" (NASB). In Luke 12:5 Jesus states that after death, Satan has power to cast man into hell, indicating that hell exists not in this life but in the afterlife.

One of the clearest teachings on hell appears in Mark 9:43-48. It is usually assumed that the hand, the foot, and the eyes are among the most priceless possessions of the body. The Lord Jesus taught here that if any one of these members were to keep us in sin and apart from the redeeming grace of God, it would be better to have them cut off or plucked out than to be cast into hell fire. In other words, as horrible as it would be to go through life maimed or crippled, that is nothing compared to the torment of hell.

Unquenchable Fire

Verse 43 of Mark 9 tells us that hell contains "fire that never shall be quenched." People often ask, "Is the fire of hell literal fire?" I believe that it is, for the effects produced by the flame duplicate those of literal fire. Furthermore, Revelation 19:20 tells us that this is a brimstone fire. Like atomic radiation, brimstone burns its way into the flesh and is excruciatingly hot. The rich man exclaimed, "I am tormented in this flame." He also called for water to "cool my tongue." Humanly speaking, nothing produces suffering comparable to fire. It is a burning, stinging, searing sensation that does not subside even after the fire has been removed. This is the Bible's picture of suffering in hell. The sobering reality is that this fire will never be removed.

Where Their Worm Dieth Not

An expression found in Mark 9:48 is most unusual. Bible scholars believe that "Hinnom" may refer to the lower end of the Valley of the Son of Hinnom which the Lord Jesus used as the symbol of eternal fire. This valley was the city dump where the dead bodies of animals were tossed. Worms were constantly growing on their subjects, and a perpetual fire was kept burning. Some have suggested that this "worm that dieth not" is the worm of conscience eating away in the heart and mind of the sufferer in hell. The gnawing reminder of his rejection of the gospel and the Savior will keep burning itself into his heart. It is bad enough to suffer the physical torments of eternal hell in the Lake of Fire, but to be constantly reminded that your own choice banished you to eternal torture must be excruciating. Lest that seem too far-fetched to you, recall what Abraham said to the rich man in Hades: "Remember that in your lifetime . . ."

No Friends in Hell

All my life I have heard men who rejected Christ say rather glibly, "I don't mind going to hell because most of my friends will be there." (Naturally, this is not a real indication of what that man feels, but a coverup of his true feelings and fears.) Those he knew on earth may well share hell with him, but I am inclined to believe that the millions of people who will populate the Lake of Fire for eternity will not enjoy fellowship. I come to this conclusion after recognizing that one of man's basic drives is for fellowship or companionship; few people enjoy being alone. By contrast, hell is a place where a man will not be permitted to enjoy things, for it is a place of torment. Thus we cannot anticipate any communication whatsoever in the Lake of Fire.

If, by any stretch of the imagination, fellowship should exist in hell, decent people will be facing a serious dilemma. Hell is not just populated by the good, clean, moral people whose main failing in life is that they have rejected Jesus Christ. It will likewise be inhabited by the grossly wicked: "murderers and sexually immoral and sorcerers and idolaters and all liars shall have their part in the lake which burns with fire and brimstone, which is the second death." This can mean only one thing: if there is fellowship at all, there will be no restraint in hell—no police force, no moral standards, no code of decency. It will be populated by all the perverted, vicious, lustful, sinful, adulterous people who have populated this earth. This will make it impossible for the "virtuous in this life" to remain virtuous in the Lake of Fire. Even if they tried to live by standards of decency, they would be overwhelmed by all of the wicked who will pursue their lusts without respectability or restraint. Degenerate people would only serve as a constant aggravation and terror to the more decent unbelievers. No wonder hell is described by the Lord Jesus Christ as a place where there will be "weeping and gnashing of teeth."

Origin of Hell

The origin and purpose of hell adds to the horror of it. It is impossible to pinpoint just when the Lake of Fire was created, but it seems from Genesis 1:1 that it was not in the original design of God, nor in his primal creative act, for we are told that "In the beginning God created the heavens and the earth" (NASB). All that follows in the chapters on creation is an expansion of verse 1, and nothing is said to indicate that any other place than the heavens and the earth was created at that time. It is interesting to note that only one earth is mentioned, whereas "heavens" is plural. This is compatible with recent discoveries made through the modern telescope that show not just one heaven, but several. The Bible mentions three heavens: the lower, the middle, and the upper. The lower heaven would be that which surrounds the earth and contains our clouds; the middle heaven is the astronomical or starry heaven; the upper heaven is, as we think of it, the heaven of God.

Why Was Hell Created?

The creation of an awesome place like the "Lake of Fire" must have been for an unusual purpose. That purpose is found in Matthew 25:41. "Then He will also say to those on the left hand, 'Depart from Me, you cursed, into the everlasting fire prepared for the devil and his angels.' " This statement made by Jesus Christ, relating to Judgment Day, points out that hell was created for the judgment of the devil and his angels. The apostle Peter sheds more light on this subject in 2 Peter 2:4: "For if God did not spare the angels who sinned, but cast them down to hell and delivered them into chains of darkness, to be reserved for judgment . . ." Because the angels sinned, they are being "reserved for judgment."

Just when these angels sinned with the devil is not absolutely certain. In the book of Job we learn that the angels were present at the original creation of the earth. It suggests that the earth was the choice dwelling place of the angels for perhaps millions of years, and then Lucifer—the greatest created being, perfect in all his ways in the day he was made, rebelled against God (Ezekiel

28:15; Isaiah 14:12-15). It is impressive to notice the number of heaven's angels that fell on that fateful day. Revelation 12:4 tells us, "And his tail drew a third of the stars of heaven and threw them to the earth." Think of it! One-third of darkness by choosing to rebel against the most high God and to follow Lucifer, the great deceiver.

Lake of Fire Not for Man

From these statements of the Lord Jesus Christ and the apostle Peter, we perceive that the "Lake of Fire" was not intended for man at all, but was really meant for the eternal punishment of supernatural beings like the devil and his angels. From the book of Revelation, particularly chapter 20, verses 11-15, it is evident that mankind will be cast into the Lake of Fire in spite of the fact that it was not originally created for him. There he will confront the indescribable misery and suffering referred to already and be numbered among the hosts of fallen supernatural beings. May the realization of the magnitude of hell have an impact on you as it had on Adolph Monad, the outstanding French preacher, who wrote: "I did everything I could to avoid seeing eternal suffering in the Word of God, but I did not succeed in it. . . .When I heard Jesus Christ declare that the wicked would go away into eternal punishment, and the righteous to eternal life, and that therefore, the sufferings of the one class would be eternal in the same sense that the felicity of the other would be . . .I gave in; bowed my head; I put my hand over my mouth; and I made myself believe in eternal suffering."

Who Will Be in Hell?

Revelation 19:20 provides the first biblical account of someone being cast into the Lake of Fire. That event takes place at the end of the tribulation period, just before the millennial kingdom begins (see chart on page 31). The Beast (or the antichrist, as he is also called), the False Prophet (his personal religious leader who tries to persuade people to worship the antichrist), and the devil (who has been the originator of the rebellion all along) cause a great insurrection at the end of the tribulation. Verse 19 shows them "gathered together to make war against Him who sat on the horse and against his army." (As we might expect, he that sat on the horse is the Lord Jesus Christ, coming with his great heavenly host.) In verse 20, both the Beast and the False Prophet are taken and "cast *alive* into the lake of fire burning with brimstone." These men—and they are only men—are thrown into the Lake of Fire and remain there until the end of the one-thousand-year kingdom of Christ, when they are seen once again. To my knowledge, there is no mention of judgment taking place for these men, and they are not included among those who are summoned from Hades at the Great White Throne Judgment. They are judged and placed into the Lake of Fire according to their works, for God is a just God, and we can depend on his justice to mete out a decree commensurate with their deeds.

Revelation 20:10 tells us that Satan joined the two already in the Lake of Fire, where they all "will be tormented day and night forever and ever." Satan will have been chained in the bottomless pit during the thousand years of peace on earth (otherwise there would be no peace), but he will be loosed thereafter for the sole purpose that he might "go out to deceive the nations which are in the four corners of the earth." He shall gather a group of people, "whose number is as the sand of the sea," to fight against the Lord at the end of the millennial period. He and his armies will be completely subdued, and then Satan too will be cast into the hottest and most grievous place in the Lake of Fire, to endure torment forever and ever.

How Long Is Forever?

"Everlasting," a concept found throughout the Bible, comes from the Hebrew word *olam* and is most often used with reference to God. Abraham called on the "everlasting God" (*olam* God). The psalmist declared, "The eternal God is our refuge, and underneath are the everlasting [*olam*] arms." The psalmist said, "Lead me in the way everlasting [*olam*]." We also find the statement, "The righteous is an everlasting [*olam*] foundation" (Proverbs 10:25) and in Daniel 12:2 we read that the resurrection in the last days will direct "some to everlasting life, and some to shame and everlasting contempt." The word "everlasting" (*olam*) causes no controversy when it refers to God. If we accept that God is everlasting or eternal because this word *olam* is applied to him, then we will have no trouble assuming that the believer has eternal life (*olam* life). Carrying this one step further, the word used to express the eternality of God and eternal life for the believer also delineates the fate of the *un*believer—everlasting contempt. Therefore we are confronted with the fact that as certain as God is eternal and believers receive eternal union with God, so the unbeliever is sentenced to eternal separation from God.

In the New Testament, the Greek word for "ever" is *aion*. It means an age, an indefinite period of time. This word, utilized frequently in conjunction with "forever," occurs thirteen times in the book of Revelation alone. If "ever" means age, then "forever and ever" obviously means "ages and ages"—the multiplication of indefinite periods of time, or time beyond our comprehension. In the book of Revelation, this expression is used nine times for the existence of God, once to express the eternal existence of the saints after death, and three times to express torment or suffering in hell for either the devil or men without Christ.

Once again, we are brought back to the unalterable conclusion that as an eternal God is "forever and ever," and the future of the Christian is "forever and ever," so the awful plight of the lost is "forever and ever."

May I pause here to point out that I find no pleasure in considering torments of the damned in hell for ages and ages. And I am confident that God does not take delight in that prospect either. I have heard men misrepresent God as gleefully banishing sinful men to hell. This is blatantly unfair and inaccurate. Personally, I believe that as the Lord Jesus sits on the Great White Throne, hot tears will course down his face as sinners are turned away because their names are not written in the Book of Life. Full of compassion, Jesus wept over the city of Jerusalem; he shed tears at the grief of Mary and Martha, and he will bewail the lot of men who slip into hell because of their rejection of him. But even his tears will not change the sobering fact that they who reject him will be cast into hell "forever and ever."

What About the Love of God?

Scripture clearly teaches that our Father is a God of love, and yet he permits untold suffering in the world. Just the other day I read of a tragic accident in which a drunk driver ran into a couple on the freeway, killing both of them and leaving five children orphaned. This incident, we must remind ourselves, was not God's fault; he permitted it as a result of human sin. That is, the willful sin of the drunk driver initiated this awful suffering. I have heard of children born with hideous deformities because of the sins of their parents. God created us as free people with the privilege of making our own choices in life. He has not put together robots programmed to love and obey him; he has implanted a choice, an opportunity to freely return his love. Does it not follow that God, who has proven his love through Jesus Christ and his death on Calvary's cross to establish his justice, will also permit men who reject his Son to suffer hell?

Truly the greatest example of the love of God is found in the death of his Son for the sins of men. He did not die for his own sins, but for the sins of the world! In this act we have the fulfillment of the verse, "For God so loved the world that He gave His only begotten Son." Is it "just" for Jesus Christ to have come and to have died if men, refusing his payment for their sins, do not have to pay the penalty themselves? Of course not! Hell is a just penalty for sin.

Why People Go to Hell

People are dispatched to hell because they are not fit to enter heaven. The Lord Jesus Christ said in John 3:3, "Most assuredly,

I say to you, unless one is born again, he cannot see the kingdom of God." "Born again" means "born from above" or "born anew," indicating that natural, physical birth is not sufficient to entitle man to see the kingdom of God. Unless a man is born again, he is "corrupt in all his deeds"; unprepared for the spiritual delights of heaven; he must spend eternity in the Lake of Fire. The apostle Paul clarified in 1 Corinthians 15:50, " . . .flesh and blood cannot inherit the kingdom of God; nor does corruption inherit incorruption." Our corrupt mortal bodies cannot dwell in heaven without contaminating it, for heaven is a perfect place.

A Christian has full assurance that he is going to heaven, not because he is naturally fit for heaven, but because he has been made fit by the new birth. This is not true for the ungodly person, who is "dead" toward God while he lives and consequently can only respond to the resurrection of the dead—or the second death.

The Savior Is Waiting

If Jesus Christ had not come into this world to die for man's sins, we would all be sent to hell. None of us is good enough for heaven. But because he loves us, Jesus paid the penalty and accepted total punishment for all of our offenses against him, thus making heaven available to us. It is not that our sins are somehow minimized or overlooked; they are simply forgiven and forgotten. Those who are foolish enough to pass up this free ticket to heaven are thereby reserving a spot in hell.

In the archives of the Supreme Court of the United States there is a record of a very strange incident that took place during the term of President Andrew Jackson. A man named George Wilson was sentenced to die "by hanging" for a crime that he had committed. Somehow the story came before the President, who granted a pardon. To everyone's amazement, Wilson tore the pardon to shreds and threw it on the floor of his cell. The ensuing legal argument concerned the validity of a pardon that was refused, and the question arose as to whether or not he should be freed or hanged. After great deliberation, the U. S. Supreme Court ruled as follows: "A pardon is a writing, the value of which is dependent upon the acceptance by the individual for whom it is intended." It was therefore decreed by the court that George Wilson be hanged until dead—not because a pardon was not offered, but because it was not accepted.

This is a perfect picture of the sinner who hears the gospel of Jesus Christ and knows that God has written a pardon for him, yet rejects him and thus forfeits his right to the pardon. If you are without the Savior today, it is because you choose to be. However, your choice to reject Jesus Christ automatically invalidates your pardon and sentences you to the Lake of Fire.

The apostle Paul once wrote, "Behold, now is the accepted time; behold, now is the day of salvation" (2 Corinthians 6:2).

CHAPTER EIGHT

THE TRUTH ABOUT OBES

By this time you have probably noticed some similarities between the out-of-the-body experiences described in Chapter One and the Bible teachings on life in the afterlife. On the other hand, you have no doubt detected several major differences. Admittedly, the Bible supplies far more information about the future activities of the dead than any other book ever written, so it is not surprising that we have uncovered an enormous amount of detail not learned in studying OBEs. In an attempt to be fair to those who accept OBEs as positive experiences inspired by God, we should examine both the similarities and differences between OBEs and biblical concepts.

Similarities Between OBEs and Bible Teaching

1) A dead person does not cease to exist. Every account includes some kind of existence after all bodily functions seem to terminate and the person is declared clinically dead. Our Lord in Luke 16:22, 23 taught that both Lazarus and the rich man continued existence immediately, one in "comfort" and one in "torment."

2) A soul-spirit seems to maintain the same characteristics after he leaves the body that he possessed while inhabiting the body. For example, he is able to "remember" even without the aid

of physical brain cells; he can also feel "comfort" and "pain" without a "heart" or what scientists term the individual's "emotional center."

3) Personhood and identity are maintained after "death." Both the Bible and the Moody-Kubler-Ross research agree that soul-spirits are the same people they were when alive.

4) There is recognition of loved ones and friends on the other side.

5) There is communication among soul-spirits in the afterlife.

6) Soul-spirits have the ability to see, think, and feel after leaving the body.

7) The soul-spirit is a temporary state. Both OBE reports and the Bible assume that the soul-spirit is not the final "trip." Both indicate that another state of existence, not clearly defined, awaits the individual. Only Scripture, however, declares a bodily resurrection, uniting the soul-spirit with a new eternal body.

Differences Between OBEs and Bible Teachings

Although a number of similarities can be listed, serious contradictions between out-of-the-body experiences and the Bible persist. In addition, several of the researchers have drawn dangerous conclusions and advanced theories that contradict the Scriptures. Consider the following:

1) God (or the "angel of light") will accept everyone, whether good or bad, into his kingdom. This is contrary to the teaching of our Lord, who said, "Therefore as the tares are gathered and burned in the fire, so it will be at the end of this age. The Son of Man will send out His angels, and they will gather out of His kingdom all things that offend, and those who practice lawlessness, and will cast them into the furnace of fire. There will be wailing and gnashing of teeth" (Matthew 13:40-43). He also explained, "Again, the kingdom of heaven is like a dragnet that was cast into the sea and gathered some of every kind, which, when it was full, they drew to shore; and they sat down and gathered the good into

vessels, but threw the bad away. So it will be at the end of the age. The angels will come forth, separate the wicked from among the just, and cast them into the furnace of fire. There will be wailing and gnashing of teeth" (Matthew 13:47-50; see also Matthew 25:41).

2) Jesus Christ is not consistently presented as unique. The roving personage of light who greets OBE travelers is never identified, nor does he identify himself; consequently each individual can select a name for this God-like being—Buddha, Mohammed, Christ or ??? By contrast, the Bible teaches that no man comes to the Father but by Jesus (John 14:6). Paul also promises that when we become "absent from the body, we are present with the Lord."

3) There is no future judgment for sin. Possibly the most dangerous teaching of OBE advocates, placing its theories in direct opposition to the Bible, is the absence of any judgment by God. As we have seen; whereas the Bible leaves no doubt about the inevitability of this judgment, for both believers and nonbelievers, the experiences of those who have returned to earthly existence record no such "balancing of the scale" of good and evil. They show everyone, regardless of deeds of faith done in this life, receiving the same benevolent treatment. In fact, in most cases the response goes beyond indifference to sin to the point of actual approval. As Dr. Moody reports, "The reward-punishment model of the afterlife is abandoned . . .even by many who had been accustomed to thinking in those terms."[1] He states that even when people were confronted with their most sinful deeds, the being they met responded with understanding and "even with humor." This totally contradicts God's character and his stated word. He sees no humor in sins that were hideous enough to require the suffering and cruel death of his only Son. Besides the obvious denial of God's integrity, this concept presents eternal dangers for men's souls. If we can anticipate a pleasant afterlife in which there is no ultimate judgment for sin, then we do not need to fear death. Fear

is not pleasant, but it is very helpful and necessary when it causes us to take a close look at the condition of our souls. Jesus warned us about the reality of hell so that we could plan to avoid it. If man can be convinced that it poses no real threat to him, he will ignore opportunities to "get right with God," thereby reserving a seat in that very place whose existence he denied.

4) Both Christians and unbelievers have the same experience in the afterlife. This OBE concept also conflicts with many Bible passages which clearly verify that "saved" and "lost" are living states in the afterlife; when death occurs, individuals proceed to different places based on their faith or lack of it. Jesus referred to the "resurrection of life" and the "resurrection of damnation" (John 5:29). Daniel, the Old Testament prophet, alluded to these two opposing places by predicting that some would awaken to everlasting contempt (Daniel 12:2). In the book of Revelation the prophet John forecast that "the blessed" (believers) would have part in "the first resurrection," while the unsaved dead would be judged and cast into hell. This is the second death.

5) OBE travelers return and are granted a second chance after death. No such teaching exists in the Bible, nor is it intimated. In fact, the "eternal death" to which the unbeliever goes is irrevocable after death. You will recall that the antichrist and false prophet in Revelation 20:10 are still there *after* 1,000 years and are joined by Satan and all the unbelievers "forever and ever."

6) When they return, some are told to warn others regarding the next life. Abraham forbade Lazarus to go back and warn the rich man's brothers. In fact, he cautioned him that it was unnecessary because if they refused to heed "Moses and the prophets" (the Bible), they wouldn't believe if one came back from the dead (Luke 16:27-31).

7) Many returnees teach that a mortal need not fear dying, for it is a pleasurable experience. That is contrary to Hebrews 10:31, which states, "It is a fearful thing to fall into the hands of the living God."

Are Explanations Possible?

None of the OBE reports in and of themselves are very convincing because they create too many unanswerable questions. For example, can the witnesses be believed? Were they hallucinating? Were they having a dream? But as I have already acknowledged, when the 150 reports of Moody are coordinated with those of Dr. Osis, Kubler-Ross, theosophists, astro-travelers and many others, it does cause one to wonder at the similarities. Admittedly, no two of Dr. Moody's travelers had exactly the same experience. However, many of them did share between eight and twelve steps in common. That phenomenon needs some explanation.

Unfortunately, since we are physical creatures and these former "dead" people are reporting events of another (spirit) dimension, we may never fully understand their origin. We can, however, offer some excellent possibilities that *may* pull the entire phenomenon back into the natural realm entirely.

Mark Albrecht and Brooks Alexander, researchers/writers for *The Journal of the Spiritual Counterfeits Project* (April 1977) have listed three thought provoking possibilities. I use them by permission and add some of my own.

1. The Physiological or Neurological Explanation.
Briefly stated, this theory would explain these experiences as having a physical basis in the nervous system. Cerebral anoxia (lack of oxygen) is known to produce hallucinations: the flashing of one's life before his or her eyes at the moment of impending death is a well-known phenomenon. Hypnosis has demonstrated that total recall of details and events in the distant past can be invoked—it is widely held that all sensory impressions are recorded on mental "film" and stored in the brain. If studies which estimate that we use only 10% of our mental capacity are correct, the other 90% must be capable of incredible things if the right "buttons" are pushed, including the virtual re-experiencing of authentic life memories. All of this is to suggest that while these experiences are real enough, they may depict subjective rather than objective reality—that they may display the potential of the human nervous system rather than the nature of the "other side." The repetition of some themes of experience (e.g., the long dark tunnel, the "being of light," etc.) may be

due to the fact that certain deep structures of the nervous system are common to all humans.

2. Utilization of Latent Psychic Human Powers Rendered Dormant by the Fall.

From a biblical perspective, it would seem logical that the 90% of mental potential that lies fallow and unused can be traced to the fall of man and the resultant curse. Scripture suggests that our spiritual powers and perceptions were severely restricted. Yet, we are made in the image of God just as Adam and Eve were, even if that image has been somewhat corroded. It is fair to assume that those latent spiritual intellectual capabilities (some may call them "psychic" powers) can be aroused by certain stimuli—a brush with death, for example. Because these latent powers are aroused in the wrong context (i.e., in our fallen moral state, apart from God), the experiences or insights generated may be garbled, conflicting or incomplete, the last three adjectives accurately describing many of Moody's and Kubler-Ross's findings. Secular psychology's multitude of theories on the subconscious and collective unconscious certainly exhibits parallels to the idea of untapped capabilities and raises the possibility of a similar understanding.

3. Voluntary or Involuntary Deception.

A third explanation, mentioned briefly above, is that of selective manipulation of some facts, exaggeration of others and perhaps some degree of outright fabrication. As we have pointed out, Moody, Kubler-Ross and Monroe all are involved in mystical experiences and have a vested interest, emotionally, ideologically and financially, in the acceptance of their views. To consider these possibilities, it is not necessary to allege conscious bad faith. People being what they are in a fallen world, it is inevitable that they will use such obscure and incomplete data as a screen upon which to project their own vision of ultimate values. In a world where facts are routinely misrepresented, taken out of context to prove any point, or just plain made up, we should at any rate caution ourselves to be skeptical, or at least discerning, especially in matters of such import as these.

4. Demonic Disguise and/or Deception.

Since the spiritual stakes are so high in this entire issue of life after death, we must also be prepared to consider one of the clearest scriptural possibilities, even though it is one of the most difficult biblical themes to handle responsibly. In view of the necromantic connections of the leading thanatologists, the obvious biblical inference must be drawn

—that there is the potential of outright demonic collusion and other-worldly manipulation of mental states.

Scientifically speaking, there is nothing to negate such a possibility. In fact, so little is known of the interrelationship between the neurological, the psychic and the spiritual that "science" would be hard put to say anything at all that was not essentially speculation. It is common knowledge that the experience of a thought or emotion is the subjective correlate of a series of electrochemical events which take place within the brain. Some psychic researchers have suggested that strong emotions facilitate telepathic "transmissions"; as Christians we assume that our thought life and emotional state affect our comprehension of God. Under the circumstances, then, it is at least reasonable to suggest that if neurological events can impinge upon the psychic and spiritual realms, the influence might run in the other direction as well, so that spiritual beings could influence the conditions of human consciousness.[2]

Personally, I think the authors are quite restrained here, for I consider their last theory the most probable explanation.

Jesus Christ is not glorified in *any* of these experiences as he would be if they were of God. The OBE reports only identify Jesus *if* the individual is a Christian or has a biblical background. Otherwise, the personage is called "angel of light," "angel of death," or a religious leader with which the individual is acquainted. When Jesus appeared to Saul on the Damascus Road (Acts 9), he identified himself, "I am Jesus whom you are persecuting." As Stephen was being stoned he recognized the Lord (Acts 7) and called him by name. By contrast, demons never glorify Jesus except under direct command. Consequently, if these confrontations with "the angel of light" do not glorify Jesus, we know they are not of God. If they are not of man—that is, a human phenomenon of the mind—there is only one other alternative: Satan. If these OBE experiences are of Satan, who is not omnipresent (everywhere present at one time), they must be the work of his demons. Thus OBE becomes demon oppression or possession.

The Demonic Communication System

It is my carefully considered opinion that out-of-the-body experiences actually happen—but no one really leaves his body. Instead, at a time of emotional or physical pressure, the normal defense mechanisms are somehow lowered and the person is vulnerable to demon oppression from which he would be ordinarily immune. These "gremlins of the mind," as Robert Louis Stevenson used to call them, can prey on the helpless victim's subconscious mind and take him through a series of events—the similarities of which may, as already mentioned, be due to the physical construction of the brain. He plays back life's circumstances, as happens in a near drowning experience, then he is mentally led into the "staging area" by the personage of love, who takes him to "a beautiful place." In truth, the individual never leaves his own body.

You may well ask, "What about the reports of those who have looked down on their own bodies and later narrated events in other rooms, like a sister crying and praying? This is really quite simple. If NBC Sports can transport me to the Orange Bowl in Miami and let me watch Terry Bradshaw and the Pittsburgh Steelers outgun Roger Staubach and the Dallas Cowboys in Superbowl XIII, though I never leave my home in San Diego thousands of miles away, why couldn't Satan's imps send a spirit video image into the subconscious mind from any place on earth—or in the universe, for that matter? Such demons, once they were able to relay messages to the defenseless mind of a "clinically dead" person through a psychic TV-like signal, could program anything they wish, and when the individual was resuscitated, he would swear that his "experience" was "real." This would certainly explain Dr. Ritchie's nine-minute trip to Norfolk, Virginia, when he "died and left his body."

When I am unconscious in sleep, I sometimes dream of weird things I never think about on the conscious level. Occasionally the dream introduces subjects with which I vigorously disagree, do not believe, or do not want to think about. I have often envisioned things that seemed graphically real but never happened in time and were never related to reality. If a person can do that during sleep, how much more would he be vulnerable if a video-inclined demon wished to take a fix on his psychic subconscious with some satanic message during an emergency-induced unconscious state? The accuracy of historical events—times, people, clothing, colors, etc.—can easily be accounted for in such a cosmic video message to the unconscious person with an "alive" mind. It would also give credence to the deceptive message that Satan's media experts want to spread—that mankind does not have to fear death, that God forgives all, etc. Such sincere "testimonials" on the Donahue or Merv Griffin shows are convincing "evidence" to millions of viewers that "out-of-the-body experiences" can dispel man's natural fear of death. Whether the reporter really knows the source of the message is irrelevant. That he *thinks* it was real helps to make his testimony convincing—and more deceptive. There are two things seriously wrong with OBE messages:

1) You don't know where they come from.

2) You don't know if they can be trusted. And since they obviously contradict the Bible, you had better be careful before you accept them!

Additional Questions Answered

Since there may be questions about my DCS (demonic communication system) theory, I will try to anticipate some of them.

1) Can Satan's imps penetrate the subconscious minds of Christians and tempt them? We are familiar with Satan's test of Job (Job 1, 2); and 1 Corinthians 10:13 acknowledges that we are all vulnerable to temptation by the devil. Interestingly enough, Moody, Osis, Kubler-Ross, and Rawlings never indicate that Christians visualized themselves going into hell. Even though a demon may try to mislead a Christian, that person is protected because, "He who is in you is greater than he who is in the world" (1 John 4:4). Evidently, the Holy Spirit and guardian angels may let Satan's demons beam their devious message into a Christian's unconscious mind—but as God built a "hedge" of protection around Job, so he guards his children from being led astray by jamming the Demonic Communication System's airwaves. After all, each of us has a guardian angel (Matthew 18:10); so pro-

tecting us at such a point of death could well be one of his assign-
ments. Remember, it is an angel that escorts us at death to God's
place of comfort (Luke 16:22).

This answers the question an airline stewardess asked me while
I was writing this book: "What about my godly grandfather who
was a Christian minister? After being pronounced dead, he went
down the long tunnel into the bright, beautiful room where a loving
person welcomed him warmly. He was then instructed to return
and finish his work. Was this demon activity?" It could have been
a demonic attempt to hook onto his unconscious mind, overruled
by the Holy Spirit or guardian angels.

Quite possibly somewhere in our psychic subconscious we all
have a frequency that is responsive to spiritual messages. Certainly all Christians are attuned to the frequency of heaven, for
they will respond to the Savior when he calls to them in the resurrection (1 Thessalonians 4:16, 17). It *may* be that God permits
angels to use that frequency in times of great distress to comfort
people, but occasionally demons try to interfere.

Some of Moody's reports by professing Christians are not scrip-
turally accurate—so they obviously are not of angelic origin.
Either those who provide accounts of biblically inaccurate experiences are not really Christian; or perhaps some Christians who
have at one time dabbled in the occult can receive a demon's
message. This explains why it is essential to "try the Spirits to
see if they are of God"; that is, to test their accuracy by the Bible.
When a person "returns to life" and reports that a well-known
Christ-rejector was waiting at the end of the tunnel to welcome
him, I become suspicious that the DCS broadcasting system does
not emanate from God.

I see no cause for Christians to be alarmed at the possibility that
Satan might accidentally hook onto their subconscious mind during
an emergency and so deceive them. Admittedly, he would like to,
but the Holy Spirit resides in us, and God has given his angels
charge over us. Either one of those protections is more than adequate as long as we do not cultivate demon communications during

our lifetime by consulting witches, Ouija boards, fortune tellers, etc.

2) You may ask, "Do Christians who really die have such DCS communications?" No one knows, but you can be sure that they will be carried by the angel to Paradise in their soul-spirit to await the resurrection day, as was Lazarus in Luke 16.

3) After returning from an out-of-the-body experience, why do the unsaved tell essentially the same story as Christians? Very simple! Satan is the Master Deceiver of man (Matthew 24:24). Our Lord called him the father of lies (John 8:44). If he can't lie to Christians by picturing them in hell, then he will deceive the lost by picturing them as going to heaven when they die, regardless of how they live.

4) "What would be the satanic purpose for such deceptions?" No doubt there are many. First, Satan destroys the credibility of God's Word, which teaches judgment, hell, and damnation for those who reject Christ. This is exactly what he said in the Garden of Eden to mother Eve, "Yea, hath God said...? Ye shall *not* surely die" (Genesis 3:1, 4b). It is just another Garden of Eden type DCS message which causes man to question God's Word.

Another purpose is to destroy man's natural fear of death. As we shall see, that is the principal danger in the whole demonic communication system being used for out-of-the-body experiences. Anyone with a comfortable feeling toward death could make the wrong decision in preparing for the next world.

Still another possibility could be that Satan wishes to herald a one-world religion based on out-of-the-body teachings—to foster an "eat, drink, and be merry" morality, and to get men more interested in hearing from OBEs than responding to the Holy Spirit and the Word of God.

5) "Would OBEs who have had these DCS messages by demon oppression tend to be more vulnerable to demon possession later?" Possibly, if they are not Christians, though not in every case. The literature of the thanatologists indicates that *most* people have only one out-of-the-body experience, and even they acknowledge that

some people later have converted to Christ. Still others have and doubtless will become willing antennae for DCS messages. Such individuals make themselves extremely vulnerable to demon possession and probably become such with their first or second willing communication after resuscitation.

6) "What is the difference between a demon possessed and a demon oppressed person?" Without going into great detail, I find the two conditions very different, although the short-term effects may be quite similar. In demon possession one or more demons are actually in the mind area of the individual and can influence or control his thinking, speech, and actions. Such is the case with mediums, mystics, and witch doctors who manifest psychic powers that defy human explanation.

Almost everyone is "oppressed" by demons at times during his lifetime, but as long as we "resist the devil," as Scripture teaches, or "give no place to the devil," or command him to leave us alone in the name of Jesus Christ, he will not enter us. (Study Ephesians 6:10-18.) Consequently, he can only tempt us or influence our thinking from the outside. In the light of my DCS theory, at a time of excruciating stress he may be able to beam a message into the mind that could provide an individual with an out-of-the-body experience.

Bible scholars generally agree that "astro-projectionists," or those who "will" their minds to the psychic or cosmic powers, are ultimately indwelt by demons, which explains why they can astro-travel at will. Swedenborg's theology, acquired on his many soul-spirit travels to "heaven and hell," is so obviously anti-biblical that we can be sure it did not emanate from God. Consequently there is only one other spiritual source to which it can be traced—Satan, via "DCS" or some such psychic mechanism.

It is well known that the more a person practices astro-travel, the easier it is to initiate and the more vivid the images become. In other words, a demon-possessed person would have many frequency channels from which to choose to beam his DCS message, whereas the ordinary person, even when "oppressed," probably only has one channel frequency to his soul-spirit, and even then he must be encouraged by the individual or take advantage of him at a time of great weakness.

7) "Do all non-Christians receive DCS messages at death?" Evidently not. Many famous unbelievers departed into the blackness of eternity, kicking and scratching in cold, naked fear. Either they received a different message from the DCS channel or they heard the true death angel that takes unrepentant people into torment upon death, much as the rich man of Luke 16 was taken.

Dr. Herbert Lockyer's interesting book, *Last Words of Saints and Sinners,* quotes some leading skeptics at death. Consider the following samples:

VOLTAIRE, the noted French infidel, had used his pen to retard and demolish Christianity. The physician who attended Voltaire at his death said that he cried out, saying:

I am abandoned by God and man! I will give you half of what I am worth if you will give me six months' life. Then I shall go to hell; and you will go with me. O Christ! O Jesus Christ!

WILLIAM POPE, who died in 1797, is said to have been the leader of a company of infidels who ridiculed everything religious. One of their exercises was to kick the Bible about the floor or tear it up. Friends who were present in his death chamber spoke of it as a scene of terror. He died crying:

I have no contrition. I cannot repent. God will damn me. I know the day of grace is past. . . .You see one who is damned forever. . . .Oh, Eternity! Eternity!. . .Nothing for me but hell. Come, eternal torments. . .I hate everything God has made, only I have no hatred for the devil—I wish to be with him. I long to be in hell. Do you not see? Do you not see him? He is coming for me.

PERIGOOD-TALLEYRAND (1754-1838), the renowned French statesman, also known as an infidel, cried:

I am suffering, Sire, the pangs of the damned.[3]

One cannot help wondering if Drs. Moody, Kubler-Ross, Osis, and other modern thanatologists included such deathbed utterances in their evaluations.

Returning to the above question, I would just add this possibility. Since less than fifty percent of those who are conscious at death have such an experience as a DCS (or, if you prefer, an OBE), not everyone has a ready demon tuned to his frequency in that moment. But you can be sure that the "Death Angel" or "Angel of Light" has a fix on the soul-spirit's frequency—depending on whether or not the person has repented of his sins and received Jesus Christ as Lord and Savior.

Eternity is one trip you prepare for in advance, whether you like it or not!

This DCS theory isn't perfect, but it is original and it does offer a plausible solution to questions raised by out-of-the-body experiences. Admittedly, it does not solve all of the problems raised by this phenomenon, but it does resolve more of them than any other theory with which I am familiar. It also explains the similarity between the ancient art of astro-projection or astro-travel and out-of-the-body experiences.

The Dangers of Thanatology

One of Dr. Moody's patients gave a public testimonial on the Merv Griffin show one evening. The following is a careful reproduction.

I had gall bladder surgery and after that I was not responding. I wasn't coming around. They rushed me back to my room, ordered X-rays. The next thing I heard was, "Catch her, she's falling!" I looked past to see who was falling. I felt arms around me. Then the next thing I heard was, "I've lost her. I can't face her daughter and tell her I've lost her."

Then he said, "Give her to the nurse. Give her oxygen." She reaches up and goes through me to get the oxygen mask to give me. I could see out in the hall with the door closed where the family had been called because they had been notified I was dying.

There had been terrific pain, but all had stopped then. It was just wonderful. No pain. Then I had what I call guides with me—people, messengers, angels. They were a presence with me. And I was not in the body. I could look back and see my body on the bed. And I felt myself in an upward motion going through this dark tunnel. And I'm coming out into a very bright light.

The colors there are magnificent. We don't have any colors here that come close. Everything here is a pale outline of what was there. The colors are more green, bluer. And music you'll never hear anything like except in heaven. There were people there. My mother and my grand-parents met me. There for a few minutes I felt, before I was really greeted by them, for once I'm me, I'm no one's dog, I'm no one's wife, I'm no one's mother, I'm me.

I met a Being of Light that I recognized as Jesus. And he loves to joke as well as anyone else. And I'd always heard that on judgment day you're going to be judged. But my whole life was flashed in front of me. What I had done and guess what? He wasn't judging me. I was doing my own judgment of myself. Whether I was happy or not.

I talked to an old girlfriend there. There was no mistake of what was being said. It was a universal language. It's more like reading the mind. You instantly know. As the thought is formed you pick up on what is being said so there is no chance of misunderstanding.

The doctor tried to resuscitate me but then he told them to quit because there wouldn't be any need to bring me back, I'd be a vegetable. But oddly enough as we were going toward the city of light I kept being told, you still have things to do, don't you want to go back? No, I didn't want to go back. But at the same time my daughter was calling. "Mom, don't leave." And my husband was saying. "Please come back. Don't go, we need you." And I finally said I would. But also at this time I had, of a moment, the whole universal knowledge. From the moment of creation, everything that has ever been, ever will be or is going to be. I can't give it to you now.

When I did make the decision to return I immediately felt myself reentering through the top of my head, going in, and the pain was terrific. My guides told me that I'd have to let the doctor know that there was reason to keep on with the resuscitation. Like move or make a sound. I chose to laugh. The doctor said, "That's the best and the poorest laugh I've ever heard."[4]

Upon hearing this testimony, Dr. Moody acknowledged that he had "encountered hundreds like it."

Since this is a typical OBE, it would be wise to determine

whether only significant dangers lie within these "transmissions" or messages from the spirit world.

1) It teaches no judgment for sin, or in the case of this woman, indicates self-judgment: "I was doing my own judgment of myself. Whether I was happy or not." We have already noted that this is at odds with biblical teachings, for Jesus Christ is the judge of all men. It not only discredits the Bible but gives men a license to sin. It removes the "fear of condemnation" which has a morally up-lifting effect on society and individuals. Whom shall we believe, this woman or Jesus Christ?

2) It removes the natural "fear of death" that motivates people to prepare to meet their Maker. As Dr. Moody admits on page 94 of his book, "Almost every person has expressed to me the thought that he is no longer afraid of death." Again on page 97 he states, "Even those who previously had some traditional convictions about the nature of the afterlife world seem to have moved away from it to some degree following their own brushes with death."

The Holy Spirit uses man's natural fear of death and eternal damnation to bring him to faith in Christ. Certainly I can testify that it was fear of death that led me to Christ. Later, of course, I learned to love God and no longer fear death. But that natural motivation can well be lessened or destroyed in people who have OBEs or in the many who read or hear about them—at their eternal peril!

3) One other statement of Dr. Moody's patient that really concerns me was her reception of "universal knowledge of creation and everything that has been and is going to be." That is revelation! And it sounds just like the Hindu mystics, illuminists, and many others of the "secret mystery" cults. What a contrast to Paul, who after his conversion spent three years studying in the desert. An Old Testament scholar, he made no such "all-knowing" claim.

In the Garden of Eden Eve succumbed to Satan's offer of "knowledge" which God had forbidden. OBEs offer man the same thing—forbidden knowledge is wrong!

OBEs and Witchcraft

Mike Warnke has been a personal friend since shortly after his conversion from witchcraft to Christ. Since he has gained far more personal knowledge of the spirit world than I have, I asked his appraisal of OBEs. Needless to say, having been a high-level leader of witchcraft on the West Coast, he had given much thought to the subject. This is the gist of our conversation.

There are two communicating spirits in this world, the Holy Spirit and Satan, or truth and error. I believe that Satan tries to counterfeit much of what God does. Just as the Holy Spirit spoke to Philip, Paul, and Peter, Satan speaks to his people, and one of his methods is out-of-the-body experiences. In my experience there are three things that OBEs have in common with witchcraft:

1) They make no allowance for the judgment of sins committed in this life—everyone inherits a bigger and better house in the afterlife.

2) They do not tell the truth about hell being a literal place. When they get into the OBE and afterlife, they find all their dead loved ones smiling and happily awaiting their arrival.

3) They teach that all religions of the world have the truth.

To my question, "Are you convinced that OBEs as popularly reported are of satanic origin," he replied, "Absolutely."

OBEs and UFOs

By this time the well-informed reader may already have noticed that OBEs are not only similar to ancient "astro-projectionists" but bear a strange likeness to UFO reports.

Several researchers have set out the basic pattern of the UFO experiences as reported by their witnesses. Although they do not compare perfectly, even a casual reading exhibits a basic similarity to the OBE. Examine the following characteristics of each.

UFOs[5]	OBEs
1. Seeing a bright light	1. "a brilliant white light appeared to me"[6] "a really brilliant light"[7] "tremendously bright"[8]

2. Hearing humming, often of a musical nature

2. "a really bad buzzing noise"[9]
"a ringing noise, very rhythmic"[10]
"a loud ringing...sort of buzzing"[11]
"I began to hear music"[12]
"like Japanese wind bells"[13]

3. Floating out of one's body

3. "could feel myself moving out of my body"[14]
"I was floating five feet above the street"[15]
"I had a floating sensation as I felt myself get out of my body"[16]

4. Moving through a tunnel or tube

4. "I was moving through this long, dark place. It seemed like a sewer or something"[17]
"I went through a dark black vacuum. You could compare it to a tunnel, I guess"[18]
"I entered head first into a narrow and very, very dark passageway"[19]
"I found myself in a tunnel—a tunnel of concentric circles"[20]

5. Approaching a door or border

5. "I saw a beautifully polished door with no knob"[21]
"I saw a fence. I wanted to reach it but was drawn back, irresistibly"[22]
"The white light said, 'Come over this line'"[23]

6. Encountering some type of being, frequently haloed or floating

6. "I didn't actually see a person in this light, and yet it has a special identity"[24]
"It was a fun person to be with. And it had a sense of humor too"[25]
"The light said, 'come with me. I want to show you something'"[26]
"I definitely felt the presence of a very powerful being there with me"[27]

7. Having telepathic communication with the being

7. "It was like talking to a person, but a person wasn't there. The light was talking to me"[28]
"The thought came to my mind. It was not earthy in the form of a question,

but I guess the connotation of it was . . .''[29]

"It wasn't a voice . . . it was more like an impression that came to me"[30]

8. Seeing a rapid review of events—as on a movie screen—in the witness' life

8. "It was like I was walking from the time of my very early life on through each year of my life right up to the present"[31]

"All of my childhood thought, my whole entire life was there at the end of the tunnel, just flashing in front of me"[32]

"I found myself in a completely black void and my whole life kind of flashed in front of me."[33] (This flashback was in the form of mental pictures.)

"It flashed before me like a motion picture that goes tremendously fast"[34]

"My life began to come like a picture in front of me, and the pictures seemed to progress through my whole life"[35]

9. Undergoing an "examination"

9. "The first thing he asked me was, 'What do you have to show me that you've done with your life?' "[36]

"The light asked me if I was ready to die . . . kind of testing me more than anything else"[37]

"The first thing he said to me was that he kind of asked me if I was ready to die, or what I had done with my life that I wanted to show him"[38]

"The voice asked me a question. And what it meant was did the kind of life I had been leading up to that point seem worthwhile"[39]

10. Receiving a message or instructions to take back to others

10. "He pointed out to me that I should try to do things for other people, to try my best"[40]

"He said he would come back for me"[41]

"He told me I would live again until my nephew grew up"[42]

11. Returning to normal life surroundings

11. Coming back to life

Although no one knows a great deal about the UFO phenomenon, many Bible scholars believe they are demonic appearances of apparitions of some kind. Certainly their theology is as confused as that of the OBEs.

Have you thought it strange that the non-spiritualist philosophy of the atheistic humanists of the forties and fifties was replaced by the occult fads of the sixties, which merged into a new interest in witchcraft and satanism in the seventies (San Diego State University now offers three units of credit for witchcraft)? This came at the same time as TM, Indian gurus, mental telepathy, renewed interest in exorcism, Oriental mysticism, Hare Krishna, Sun Myung Moon, an increase in UFO citings, and the currently popular fad of the out-of-the-body experiences.

What single common denominator do all these groups, including the humanists, have in common? They reject the God of the Bible! This means they are left without absolute answers to the questions: "Where did we come from?" and "Why are we here?" or "What is right and wrong?" Even more important, they have no absolute instruction about life after death. Consequently they are vulnerable to any man-made pipe dream and easily fall prey to the master deceiver's every delusion. Interestingly enough, they disbelieve in Satan and ridicule those who accept such a concept—but that doesn't keep them from swallowing his deceptive teaching.

The sad part of it all is that these "no absolute" humanists with their academic degrees serve as the religious high priests who are leading millions away from God and the "peace" he offers to mankind. They conduct their followers into an amoral or immoral life style that not only confuses a man's present life but condemns him in the next. No wonder such people increasingly resort to tranquilizers, sedatives, drugs, and alcohol.

These high priests of humanism have not been able to provide one important service for their followers: prepare them for the ultimate trip of death. Why? They cannot impart what they do not know. Humanists ask endless questions and offer groundless theories but are incapable of satisfying their followers in the hour of death.

All prophecy students are aware that just as demon activity significantly increased before the first coming of Christ, so it will intensify prior to his second coming. The writings of both Peter and Paul attest to this. In the book of Revelation the antichrist even tries to duplicate the miracles of Jesus to the point of raising the dead. The rise in "spiritualistic" cults mentioned above, an obvious increase in demonic activity, could very well mean that the coming of Christ is closer than most people realize.

If ever there was a time when men needed to put their trust in the Word of God, which Jesus said would never pass away, it is today. In an age without absolutes, we have one absolute—God's Word. It alone offers a true glimpse of life in the afterlife.

Faith Is Its Own Reward

Space does not permit reporting the many stories of Christians who came to the "moment of death" when they were beyond the help of human hands, only to return to strength and life. But I would like to share a couple of them.

Dr. David Cavin, a pastor friend, had a heart attack while preaching one Sunday morning in the _____ Baptist Church of Ft. Worth Texas. Three times he stopped breathing before the ambulance arrived, and only by the grace of God and the mouth-to-mouth resuscitation of one of his church members is he alive today. He describes his "OBE" as a very pleasurable sensation of "floating freely upward in a white box and suddenly being jerked back to earth." His first sight from the stretcher was the U. S. flag against the blue sky. But the thing that sticks in his memory most is the *disappointment* he felt in coming back to life!

Pastor Cavin was and is a very happy and fulfilled man. He

enjoys the love of a beautiful Christian wife and three strikingly attractive children who love the Lord. He is in the prime of life, and his thriving congregation loves him dearly. Yet he was disappointed at returning to this life.

His experience should teach us something! Consider the following:

1. Christians do not need to fear death.
   "Yea though I walk through the valley of the shadow of death, I will fear no evil: for thou art with me . . ." (Psalm 23:4).

2. God has an indescribably beautiful existence planned for those who love him.
   "Eye has not seen, nor ear heard, nor have entered into the heart of man the things which God has prepared for those who love Him" (1 Corinthians 2:9).

3. No man is certain of life; death can take any of us suddenly and without warning.
   "Prepare to meet thy God" (Amos 4:12).

4. If you have not invited Jesus Christ into your life, you need to do so today.
   "Behold, I stand at the door and knock. If anyone hears My voice and opens the door, I will come in to him and dine with him, and he with Me" (Revelation 3:20).

Who Strengthened Aljeana?

"The Lord Stood by Me"

Aljeana Kole was the beautiful on-stage assistant to her master illusionist husband Andre. After their conversion to Christ they toured the world, using their "magic" demonstrations to attract people to a clear presentation of the gospel of Christ. Thousands attended their presentations, and hundreds received their Savior at the close of the performances. When we invited them to our church on one occasion, they were a great blessing to the congregation.

In 1974 Aljeana was informed by her doctors that she had cancer and would live only a few months longer. Those physicians didn't recognize, of course, that for a Christian, life in the afterlife is "eternal life." These two servants of God and their children gave glowing testimony of God's sustaining power during Aljeana's last days. In a tract Andre beautifully describes God's supply of Aljeana's final earthly needs.

A few weeks before Aljeana's death there was a point when it looked like she was going to die. For several days she had been in a semi-coma. She could no longer eat, talk or respond in any way. The doctor said she could expire at any moment. However, he asked my permission to try one last thing. He said it was very possible that she would not survive what he had in mind, but since she was at the point of death anyway it was worth a try. I gave him permission to perform the minor bit of surgery, and as a result, there was a remarkable recovery for a few days.

As soon as she came out of the coma, one of the first things she said was, "Who was the man that was with me all the time?" As we questioned her further, she said there was a young man that stood by her bed and never left her during the critical days following surgery. In her words, "He seemed to have a special feeling for me, and when the pain was very bad he would hold my hand and comfort me. I don't think I could have made it without him." When asked if he were still there, she said, "No, he left yesterday morning." The morning she referred to was the time when she started to recover from the surgery. That day we received a card in the mail with a Bible verse, "The Lord stood with me, and strengthened me" (2 Timothy 4:17).

I would hesitate to jump to any conclusions in trying to explain this experience, but I have often wondered if God allowed Aljeana to return to us just so we might know the extent of His care for His children who have accepted Him into their lives during their final hours. The Bible says, "His loved ones are very precious to him and he does not lightly let them die" (Psalm 116:15). The Bible also teaches that when we, as believers, come to die, the angels will be there to carry us into the presence of God (Luke 16:22). We tried to get her to tell us more about this experience, but she never seemed to want to talk anymore about it. However, a few weeks later her life once again began to grow dim. I had mixed emotions when she quietly said to us one night, "Do you remember the man I told you about a few weeks ago?" We said, "Yes," and she replied, "He has come back, and I am glad he is here." Aljeana never recovered again.[43]

"We are confident, I say, and well-pleased rather to be absent from the body and to be present with the Lord" (2 Corinthians 5:8).

This is not only the apostle Paul's confident attitude toward leaving this earthly scene in what non-believers call "death," but the confident expectation of all Christians.

In the words of the One who really knew about the afterlife, Jesus Christ:

"I am the resurrection and the life. He who believes in Me, though he may die, he shall live. And whoever lives and believes in Me shall never die. Do you believe this?" (John 11:25, 26).

Regardless of what we *think* happens after we die, there is an absolutely reliable source by which we can *know* exactly what to expect. This source is God and his revealed Word to us—the Bible. Since our eternity is at stake, doesn't it make sense to heed the words of him who is alive from everlasting to everlasting?

For the person who has become right with God through acceptance of his Son's death on the cross, there need be no fear of death. He can look forward to a glorious, indescribable existence planned for him from the beginning of the world!

NOTES

CHAPTER ONE

[1]Mark Albrecht and Brooks Alexander, "Thanatology: Death and Dying," *Spiritual Counterfeits Project,* No. I (1977), p. 5.

[2]George B. Ritchie and Elizabeth Sherrill, *Return from Tomorrow* (Carmel, New York: Guideposts, 1978), pp. 38-41, 97-99.

[3]Raymond Moody, *Life After Life* (Covington, Georgia: Mockingbird Books, (1975) pp. 14, 15.

[4]*Ibid.,* pp. 21-23.

[5]*Ibid.,* pp. 35, 36.

[6]Archie Matson, *Afterlife* (New York: Harper and Row, 1975), pp. 17-19.

[7]*Ibid.,* p. 29.

[8]*Ibid.,* pp. 25-27.

[9]J. C. Pollock, *Moody* (New York: Macmillan Co., 1963), p. 316, as quoted in *Beyond Death's Door,* by Maurice Rawlings, M. D.

[10]Maurice Rawlings, *Beyond Death's Door* (Nashville: Thomas Nelson Inc.), pp. 17-20.

[11]Moody, p. 17.

[12]Mike Warnke, *The Satan Seller* (Plainfield, N. J.: Logos International, 1972), p. 87.

[13]Matson, p. 55.

[14]*Ibid.,* p. 64.

[15]*Ibid.,* pp. 69, 70.

CHAPTER EIGHT

[1]Raymond Moody, *Life After Life* (Covington, Georgia: Mockingbird Books, 1975), p. 97.

[2]Mark Albrecht and Brooks Alexander, "Thanatology: Death and Dying," *Spiritual Counterfeits Project,* No. I (1977), pp. 7, 8.

[3]Herbert Lockyer, *Last Words of Saints and Sinners* (Grand Rapids, Michigan: Kregel Publications, 1969), pp. 132, 133.

[4]Stephen Board, "Light at the End of the Tunnel," *Eternity* magazine, July, 1977, p. 14.

[5]Joel Greenberg, "Close Encounters Are in the Mind," *Science News,* Feb., 1979, pp. 106, 107.

[6]Moody, p. 75.

[7]*Ibid.,* p. 77.

[8]*Ibid.,* p. 63.

[9]*Ibid.,* p. 29.

[10]*Ibid.,* p. 31.

[11]*Ibid.,* p. 30.

[12]*Ibid.,* p. 30.

[13]*Ibid.,* p. 30.

[14]*Ibid.,* p. 36.

[15]*Ibid.,* p. 37.

[16]*Ibid.,* p. 38.

[17]*Ibid.,* p. 31.

[18]*Ibid.,* p. 32.

[19]*Ibid.,* p. 33.

[20]*Ibid.,* p. 33.

[21]*Ibid.,* p. 77.

[22]*Ibid.,* p. 74.

[23]*Ibid.,* p. 75.

[24]*Ibid.,* p. 63.

[25]*Ibid.,* p. 64.

[26]*Ibid.,* p. 102.

[27]*Ibid.,* p. 70.

[28]*Ibid.,* p. 64.

[29]*Ibid.,* p. 63.

[30]*Ibid.,* pp. 103, 104.

[31]*Ibid.,* p. 66.

[32]*Ibid.,* p. 69.

[33]*Ibid.,* pp. 69, 70.

[34]*Ibid.,* p. 70.

[35]*Ibid.,* p. 71.

[36]*Ibid.,* pp. 65, 66.

[37]*Ibid.,* p. 64.

[38]*Ibid.,* p. 61.

[39]*Ibid.,* p. 61.

[40]*Ibid.,* p. 64.

[41]*Ibid.,* p. 96.

[42]*Ibid.,* p. 106.

[43]Andre Kole, from the tract, "Victory Over Death."